The Father's Love Is Unconditional

I pray that this book will be a blessing to your soul. God loves you! Thank you,

Darlene Dennard

DARLENE DENNARD

ISBN 978-1-0980-9553-6 (paperback)
ISBN 978-1-0980-9554-3 (digital)

Christian Faith Publishing
832 Park Avenue
Meadville, PA 16335
www.christianfaithpublishing.com

Scriptures are taken from Holman Rainbow Study Bible, New International Version, and the Amplified Bible Version.

Printed in the United States of America

Jesus answered, "It is written: man shall not live on bread alone, but on every word that comes from the mouth of God."

—Matthew 4:4

Contents

Acknowledgments

I would like to thank my Heavenly Father and his Son Jesus Christ, for guiding me by his Spirit and giving me the desire and wisdom to write this book, expressing his unconditional love for you through the teaching of his Word.

To the pastors, teachers, and all ministry gifts, I am very grateful to God for placing each and every one of you in my life. And for all who has imparted in me the wisdom and teaching of God's Word, thank you.

To my husband, Craig, and my daughters Keena, Tyeasha, and Deasia; son Davon; and grandsons Jesse, Logan, and little Tyrone; granddaughter Israel, I thank God for my family. They have truly been a blessing to me and always encouraging me to follow my dreams. I love you all to life.

Family and friends, to everyone who has inspired me in anyway on my life journey. I thank you all for the love and support that you have shown me. May God continue to bless each of you on your journey as well.

Special thanks to Mrs. Jannie and Marcella, my sisters in Christ for always being there for me in time of need. It has been a blessing having you in my life.

Last but not least, I would like to give honor and respect to my mother and father who have went home to be with the Lord. I want to thank them for teaching me how to love and respect others. I remember an expression of my mother, "Manners will take you where money won't." I love and miss you very much!

Introduction

In this book you will learn all about the Father God and his beloved Son, Jesus Christ, how he demonstrated his (*agape, selfless, unconditional love*), which is the highest form of love for you and his desire for you to experience that passionate love in your life. John 3:16–17 says, "For God so loved the world that he gave his one and only Son, that whoever believes in him shall not perish but have eternal life. For God did not send his Son into the world to condemn the world, but to save the world through him."

My brothers and sisters, I am glad that we have the opportunity to talk about this today because I want you to know how much the Father loves you. It is by and through believing on and having faith in his Son's grace (undeserved, unearned, and unmerited favor) alone that you have access to his love. I believe this is the reason so many of you stray away from God and attend church—thinking that you are not good enough and you have to get rid of all your sins before coming to God who is our loving Father. Nothing could be farther from the truth; we cannot save ourselves. When I started watching other ministry gifts on television teaching the Word of God like I have never heard before, I came across this one pastor teaching about the grace of God and the power to reign in life is based entirely on Jesus and him alone. Once I received the knowledge about the gift of *no condemnation* to those who are in Christ Jesus and my *righteousness* is in him, I started renewing my mind with the word of God.

I also learned that all my past, present, and future sins has already been forgiven by the blood of Jesus and his finished work on the cross. That was a big one for me. I thought that every time I missed it with God, he was going to punish me. I started studying the scriptures even more. I found out that the Father has already accepted me through his Son, and I am his beloved. I wanted to share this good news with you because it is the reason Jesus died. I believe it is safe to say that real genuine love of God is spiritual and comes from the inside out and not outside in.

I realize that everyone is looking for love in life one way or another. Because you were created by God who is love, it is only natural for you to desire that love—which is patient, kind, faithful, gentle, and peace. When you are born again, you are operating from a different kingdom, which is not of this world. I pray that you will receive this knowledge and wisdom of God on how you were created to love by renewing your mind to the Word of God and applying it to your daily life. Knowing how much the Father loves you is very important to having a personal relationship with him. All relationship should be based on real love and acceptance, not on performance. The only way you are going to overcome any situation or circumstances in your life is by knowing who you are in Christ and receiving your inheritance so that you would not operate beneath your privileges. Learn to live out of God's love for you.

IT'S
LOVE
FROM THE BEGINNING
AND
IT'S
LOVE
TO
THE
END

The Father's Love Letter to You

Beloved,

I just wanted to let you know how special you are to me and that you are always on my mind. I think about you all the time. Before the creation of the world, you were in my thoughts. Before you were in your mother's womb, I knew you, and I have fearfully and wonderfully made you. I have made you in my image and in my likeness to rule over the earth to be fruitful and to increase. I have given you, my beloved, the power, authority, and ability that you need in life. I will continually fill you with my knowledge, wisdom, and understanding; and I have given you of my Spirit so that you may live a life worthy to me and pleasing in every way because I have chosen you before the world begin. Beloved, I know the plans I have for you, plans to prosper you and not to harm you and plans to give you hope and a future. All I ask of you my beloved is to hear my voice and listen to what I am saying to you. Believe and trust in me and you will never be ashamed. For I am the Father of compassion and all comfort. I am he who forgives all your sins and heals all your diseases, who redeems your life from the pit, and he who crowns you with love and compassion. I am he who satisfies your desires with good things so that your youth is renewed like the eagle's.

I am good, and my love endures forever. My faithfulness continues through all generations. My beloved, I will protect you. I will be with you in trouble. I will deliver you and honor you with long life. I will satisfy you. I am a Father to the fatherless, a defender to the oppressed and widows. I am your refuge and strength, an ever-present help in trouble. Be still and know that I am your Father. I am close to the brokenhearted and saves those who are crushed in spirit. Taste and see that I am good. Blessed is the one who takes refuge in me. The earth is full of my unfailing love. I will instruct you and teach you in the way you should go. I will counsel you with my loving eye on you. My unfailing love surrounds the one who trusts in me. I will show you the wonders of my love. From heaven I am the Father who looks down and sees all mankind; from my dwelling place, I watch all who lives on earth.

I am he who forms the hearts of all. I consider everything they do. Surely my goodness and love will follow you all the days of your life. I am your Father. My ways are perfect, and my word is flawless. I shield all who take refuge in me. I turn your darkness into light, for I am a sun and a shield, I bestow favor and honor. No good thing will I withhold from those whose walk is blameless. I am forgiving and abounding in love to all who call on me. My law is perfect, refreshing the soul. My statutes are trustworthy, making wise the simple; my precepts are right, giving joy to the heart. I will keep you as the apple of my eye. My beloved, walk in the ways of my love. Love one another as I have loved you.

Yours truly,
YOUR HEAVENLY FATHER

You
Were
Created
by
Love
for
Love
in
Love
To
Love

The Father of Love Creates

You were created to speak and call forth things just like your Father God and his Son Jesus, whom from the beginning created everything by his Word. John 1:1–3 says, "In the beginning was the Word, and the Word was with God, and the Word was God." He [the Word] was with God in the beginning. Through him [the Word] all things were made; without him, [the Word] nothing was made that has been made. Notice that the scripture calls the Word he. I am going to show you that Jesus is the Word of God, and everything was created by him. The Son is the image of the invisible God, the firstborn over all creation. For in him all things were created: things in heaven and on earth, visible and invisible, whether thrones or powers or rulers or authorities—all things have been created through him and for him. He is before all things, and in him all things hold together.

Jesus said that "I and my Father are one." Revelation 19:13 says his name is the Word of God. I said all this to let you know how powerful your words are and that they have creative abilities. When speaking, you are creating; and it does not matter if you are speaking good or bad things. Your words are seeds, and when it is planted, it grows up to mostly whatever you are seeing in your life. Genesis 1 let us know whatever God said he saw, and it was very good.

> From the fruit of their mouth a person's stomach is filled with the harvest of their lips they are satisfied. The tongue has the power of life and death, and those who love it will eat its fruit. (Proverbs 18:20-21)

As you can see just from these scriptures, what you say really matters. What I wanted you to see is that your Father God has made you to operate just like him, calling things forth from the invisible to the visible and you are doing it without even realizing it. There is so much I can say on this subject, but I am going to leave that for another time. I just wanted you to see how everything was created by the Father and his Son, the Word. By the word of the LORD, the heavens were made; for he spoke, and it came to be he commanded and it stood firm. Your word is a lamp for my feet, a light on my path. Every word of God is flawless. The earth is full of his unfailing love.

THE
FATHER
FORGIVES
MAN
THROUGH
FAITH
IN
JESUS
CHRIST

It is Jesus's blood alone that saves you; the Father sees that as faith.

The Father Forgives Man through Faith in Jesus Christ

Therefore, since we have been justified through faith, we have peace with God through our Lord Jesus Christ,[1]

"For we maintain that a person is justified by faith apart from the works of the law."[2]

Through whom we have gained access by faith into this grace in which we now stand. And we boast in the hope of the glory of God.[3]

"For through him we both have access to the Father by one Spirit."[4]

Paul said, "Now, brothers and sisters, I want to remind you of the gospel I preached to you, which you received and on which you have taken your stand."[5]

"But Christ is faithful as the Son over God's house. And we are his house, if indeed we hold firmly to our confidence and the hope in which we glory."[6]

Not only so, but we also glory in our sufferings because we know that suffering produces perseverance.[7]

---

[1] Romans 5:1
[2] Romans 3:28
[3] Romans 5:2
[4] Ephesians 2:18
[5] 1 Corinthians 15:1
[6] Hebrews 3:6
[7] Romans 5:3

"Rejoice and be glad, because great is your reward in heaven, for in the same way they persecuted the prophets who were before you."[8]

Consider it pure joy, my brothers and sisters, whenever you face trials of many kinds, because you know that the testing of your faith produces perseverance[9];

Perseverance, character; and character, hope.[10]

And hope does not put us to shame because God's love has been poured out into our hearts through the Holy Spirit, who has been given to us.[11]

"I eagerly expect and hope that I will in no way be ashamed; but will have sufficient courage so that now, as always, Christ will be exalted in my body, whether by life or by death."[12]

"Exalted to the right hand of God, he has received from the Father the promised Holy Spirit and has poured out what you now see and hear."[13]

You see, at just the right time, when we were still powerless, Christ died for the ungodly.[14]

"But when the set time had fully come, God sent his Son, born of a woman, born under the law."[15]

"He was delivered over to death for our sins and was raised to life for our justification."[16]

But God demonstrates his own love for us in this: while we were still sinners, Christ died for us.[17]

"Greater love has no one than this: to lay down one's life for one's friends."[18]

---

8   Matthew 5:12
9   James 1:2-3
10   Romans 5:4
11   Romans 5:5
12   Philippians 1:20
13   Acts 2:33
14   Romans 5:6
15   Galatians 4:4
16   Romans 4:25
17   Romans 5:8
18   John 15:13

"For Christ also suffered once for sins, the righteous for the unrighteous, to bring you to God. He was put to death in the body but made alive in the Spirit."[19]

Since we have now been justified by his blood, how much more shall we be saved from God's wrath through him![20]

"God presented Christ as a sacrifice of atonement, through the shedding of his blood to be received by faith. He did this to demonstrate his righteousness, because in his forbearance, he had left the sins committed beforehand unpunished."[21]

"The wrath of God is being revealed from heaven against all the godlessness and wickedness of people, who suppress the truth by their wickedness."[22]

For if, while we were God's enemies, we were reconciled to him through the death of his Son, how much more, having been reconciled, shall we be saved through his life![23]

"As far as the gospel is concerned, they are enemies for your sake; but as far as election is concerned, they are loved on account of the patriarchs."[24]

"And you, that were sometime alienated and enemies in your mind by wicked works, yet now hath to reconciled."[25]

"All this is from God, who reconciled us to himself through Christ and gave us the ministry of reconciliation—that God was reconciling the world to himself in Christ, not counting people's sins against them. And he has committed to us the message of reconciliation."[26]

---

[19] 1 Peter 3:18
[20] Romans 5:9
[21] Romans 3:25
[22] Romans 1:18
[23] Romans 5:10
[24] Romans 11:28
[25] Colossians 1:21 (KJV)
[26] 2 Corinthians 5:18-19

"And through him to reconcile to himself all things, whether things on earth or things in heaven, by making peace through his blood, shed on the cross."[27]

"But now he has reconciled you by Christ's physical body through death to present you holy in his sight, without blemish and free from accusation."[28]

"Who then is the one who condemns? No one. Christ Jesus who died more than that, who was raised to life is at the right hand of God and is also interceding for us."[29]

Not only is this so, but we also boast in God through our Lord Jesus Christ, through whom we have now received reconciliation.[30]

"For it is by grace you have been saved, through faith, and this is not from yourselves, it is the gift of God."[31]

"Now faith is the confidence in what we hope for and assurance about what we do not see."[32]

"By faith we understand that the universe was formed at God's command, so that what is seen was not made; out of what was visible."[33]

"And without faith, it is impossible to please God because anyone who comes to him must believe that he exists and that he rewards those who earnestly seek him."[34]

---

[27] Colossians 1:20
[28] Colossians 1:22
[29] Romans 8:34
[30] Romans 5:11
[31] Ephesians 2:8
[32] Hebrews 11:1
[33] Hebrews 11:3
[34] Hebrews 11:6

THE
FATHER
GIVES
LIFE
THROUGH
HIS
SON
JESUS
CHRIST

You will reign in life when you believe and receive everything that Jesus has accomplished for us on the cross.

The Father Gives Life through His Son Jesus Christ

"Therefore, just as sin entered the world through one man, and death through sin, and in this way, death came to all people, because all sinned."[35]

"For since death came through a man, the resurrection of the dead comes also through a man. For as in Adam all die, so in Christ all will be made alive."[36]

"But you must not eat from the tree of the knowledge of good and evil, for when you eat from it you will certainly die."[37]

"By the sweat of your brow, you will eat your food until you return to the ground, since from it you were taken; for dust you are and to dust you will return."[38]

"For the wages of sin is death, but the gift of God is eternal life in Christ Jesus our Lord."[39]

"To be sure, sin was in the world before the law was given, but sin is not charged against anyone's account where there is no law."[40]

"Because the law brings wrath. And where there is no law there is no transgression."[41]

---

[35] Romans 5:12
[36] 1 Corinthians 15:21-22
[37] Genesis 2:17
[38] Genesis 3:19
[39] Romans 6:23
[40] Romans 5:13
[41] Romans 4:15

"Nevertheless, death reigned from the time of Adam to the time of Moses, even over those who did not sin by breaking a command, as did Adam, who is a pattern of the one to come."[42]

"It is written: 'The first man Adam became a living being,' the last Adam, a life-giving spirit."[43]

"But the gift is not like the trespass. For if the many died by the trespass of the one man, how much more did God's grace and the gift that came by the grace of one man, Jesus Christ, overflow to the many!"[44]

"No! We believe it is through the grace of our Lord Jesus that we are saved, just as they are."[45]

"Nor can the gift of God be compared with the result of one man's sin: the judgment followed one sin and brought condemnation, but the gift followed many trespasses and brought justification."[46]

"For if, by the trespass of the one man, death reigned through that one man, how much more will those who receive God's abundant provision of grace and of the gift of righteousness reign in life through the one man, Jesus Christ!"[47]

"Consequently, just as one trespass resulted in condemnation for all people, so also one righteous act resulted in justification and life for all people."[48]

"He was delivered over to death for our sins and was raised to life for our justification."[49]

"For just as through the disobedience of the one man the many were made sinners, so also through the obedience of the one man the many will be made righteous."[50]

---

[42] Romans 5:14
[43] 1 Corinthians 15:45
[44] Romans 5:15
[45] Acts 15:11
[46] Romans 5:16
[47] Romans 5:17
[48] Romans 5:18
[49] Romans 4:25
[50] Romans 5:19

"And being found in appearance as a man, he humbled himself by becoming obedient to death even death on the cross!"[51]

"The law was brought in so that the trespass might increase. But where sin increased, grace increased, all the more."[52]

"What shall we say, then? Is the law sinful? Certainly not! Nevertheless, I would not have known what sin was, had it not been for the law. For I would not have known what coveting really was if the law had not said, 'You shall not covet'."[53]

"But sin, seizing the opportunity afforded by the commandment, produced in me every kind of coveting. For apart from the law, sin was dead."[54]

"Why, then, was the law given at all? It was added because of transgressions until the Seed to whom the promise referred had come. The law was given through angels and entrusted to a mediator."[55]

"The promises were spoken to Abraham and to his seed. Scripture does not say and to seeds, meaning many people, but and to your seed, meaning one person, who is Christ."[56]

"What I mean is this: The law, introduced 430 years later, does not set aside the covenant previously established by God and thus do away with the promise. For if the inheritance depends on the law, then it no longer depends on the promise; but God in his grace gave it to Abraham through a promise."[57]

"Now we know that whatever the law says, it says to those who are under the law, so that every mouth may be silenced and the whole world held accountable to God. Therefore no one will be declared righteous in God's sight by the works of the law; rather, through the law we become conscious of our sin."[58]

---

[51] Philippians 2:8
[52] Romans 5:20
[53] Romans 7:7
[54] Romans 7:8
[55] Galatians 3:19
[56] Galatians 3:16
[57] Galatians 3:17-18
[58] Romans 3:19-20

"Before the coming of this faith, we were held in custody under the law, locked up until the faith that was to come would be revealed. The law was our guardian until Christ came that we might be justified by faith. Now that this faith has come, we are no longer under a guardian."[59]

"In Christ Jesus you are all children of God through faith."[60]

"Even though I (Paul) was once a blasphemer and a persecutor and a violent man, I was shown mercy because I acted in ignorance and unbelief. The grace of our Lord was poured out on me abundantly, along with the faith and love that are in Christ Jesus."[61]

"So that, just as sin reigned in death, so also grace might reign through righteousness to bring eternal life through Jesus Christ our Lord."[62]

---

[59] Galatians 3:23-25
[60] Galatians 3:26
[61] 1 Timothy 1:13-14
[62] Romans 5:21

BE
DEAD
TO
SIN
AND
LIVE
A
LIFE
IN
CHRIST

You have been redeemed from the curse of the law. You are now the righteousness of Father God through Jesus Christ his Son.

Be Dead to Sin and Live a Life in Christ

"What shall we say, then? Shall we go on sinning so that grace may increase?"[63]

"But if our unrighteousness brings out God's righteousness more clearly, what shall we say? That God is unjust in bringing his wrath on us? Paul said (I am using a human argument.) Certainly not! If that were so, how could God judge the world?"[64]

"Why not say, as some slanderously claim that we say. "Let us do evil that good may result?" Their condemnation is just!"[65]

"By no means! We are those who have died to sin; how can we live in it any longer?"[66]

"For you died, and your life is now hidden with Christ in God."[67]

"Put to death, therefore, whatever belongs to your earthly nature: sexual immorality, impurity, lust, evil desires and greed, which is idolatry."[68]

"'He himself bore our sins' in his body on the cross, so that we might die to sins and live for righteousness; 'by his wounds you have been healed'."[69]

---

[63] Romans 6:1
[64] Romans 3:5-6
[65] Romans 3:8
[66] Romans 6:2
[67] Colossians 3:3
[68] Colossians 3:5
[69] 1 Peter 2:24

"Don't you know that all of us who were baptized into Christ Jesus were baptized into his death?"[70]

"Therefore, go and make disciples of all nations, baptizing them in the name of the Father and of the Son and of the Holy Spirit."[71]

"We were therefore buried with him through baptism into death in order that, just as Christ was raised from the dead through the glory of the Father, we too may live a new life."[72]

"Having been buried with him in baptism, in which you were also raised with him through your faith in the working of God, who raised him from the dead."[73]

"But now, by dying to what once bound us, we have been released from the law so that we serve in the new way of the Spirit, and not in the old way of the written code."[74]

"Neither circumcision nor uncircumcision means anything; what counts is the new creation."[75]

"You were taught with regard, to your former way of life, to put off your old self, which is being corrupted by its deceitful desires; to be made new in the attitude of your minds; and to put on the new self, created to be like God in true righteousness and holiness."[76]

"Since then, you have been raised with Christ, set your hearts on things above, where Christ is, seated at the right hand of God. Set your minds on things above, not on earthly things."[77]

"And have put on the new self, which is being renewed in knowledge in the image of its Creator."[78]

"For if we have been united with him in a death like his, we will certainly also be united with him in a resurrection like his."[79]

---

[70] Romans 6:3
[71] Matthew 28:19
[72] Romans 6:4
[73] Colossians 2:12
[74] Romans 7:6
[75] Galatians 6:15
[76] Ephesians 4:22-24
[77] Colossians 3:1-2
[78] Colossians 3:10
[79] Romans 6:5

"We always carry around in our body the death of Jesus, so that the life of Jesus may also be revealed in our body."[80]

"For we know that our old self was crucified with him so that the body ruled by sin might be done away with, that we should no longer be slaves to sin because anyone who has died has been set free from sin."[81]

"I have been crucified with Christ and I no longer live, but Christ lives in me. The life I now live in the body, I live by faith in the Son of God, who loved me and gave himself for me."[82]

"Since you died with Christ to the elemental spiritual forces of this world, why, as though you still belonged to the world, do you submit to its rules:"[83]

"Now if we died with Christ, we believe that we will also live with him."[84]

"For we know that since Christ was raised from the dead, he cannot die again; death no longer has mastery over him."[85]

"But God raised him from the dead, freeing him from the agony of death, because it was impossible for death to keep its hold on him."[86]

"I am the Living One; I was dead, and now look, I am alive for ever and ever! And I hold the keys of death and Hades."[87]

"The death he died, he died to sin once for all; but the life he lives, he lives to God."[88]

"In the same way, count yourselves dead to sin but alive to God in Christ Jesus."[89]

---

[80] 2 Corinthians 4:10
[81] Romans 6:6-7
[82] Galatians 2:20
[83] Colossians 2:20
[84] Romans 6:8
[85] Romans 6:9
[86] Acts 2:24
[87] Revelation 1:18
[88] Romans 6:10
[89] Romans 6:11

"Therefore, do not let sin reign in your mortal body so that you obey its evil desires."[90]

"Do not offer any part of yourself to sin as an instrument of wickedness, but rather offer yourselves to God as those who have been brought from death to life; and offer every part of yourself to him as an instrument of righteousness."[91]

"For when we were in the realm of the flesh, the sinful passions aroused by the law were at work in us, so that we bore fruit for death."[92]

"Therefore, I urge you, brothers and sisters, in view of God's mercy, to offer your bodies as a living sacrifice, holy and pleasing to God this is your true and proper worship. Do not conform to the pattern of this world but be transformed by the renewing of your mind. Then you will be able to test and approve what God's will is his good, pleasing and perfect will."[93]

"For sin shall no longer be your master; because you are not under the law, but under grace."[94]

"But if you are led by the Spirit, you are not under the law."[95]

"And all are justified freely by his grace through the redemption that came by Christ Jesus."[96]

---

[90] Romans 6:12
[91] Romans 6:13
[92] Romans 7:5
[93] Romans 12:1-2
[94] Romans 6:14
[95] Galatians 5:18
[96] Romans 3:24

THERE
ARE
HEAVENLY
BODIES
AND
EARTHLY
BODIES

There are also heavenly bodies and there are earthly bodies;
but the splendor of the heavenly bodies is one kind,
and the splendor of the earthly bodies is another.

There Are Heavenly Bodies and Earthly Bodies

"But if it is preached that Christ has been raised from the dead, how can some of you say that there is no resurrection of the dead? If there is no resurrection of the dead, then not even Christ has been raised. And if Christ has not been raised [Paul] said our preaching is useless and so is your faith."[97]

"But someone will ask, 'How are the dead raised? With what kind of body will they come?'."[98]

"He asked me, Son of man, can these bones live?"[99]

"How foolish! What you sow does not come to life unless it dies."[100]

"You foolish people! Did not the one who made the outside make the inside also?"[101]

"Very truly I tell you, unless a kernel of wheat falls to the ground and dies, it remains only a single seed. But if it dies, it produces many seeds."[102]

"When you sow, you do not plant the body that will be, but just a seed, perhaps of wheat or of something else."[103]

---

[97] 1 Corinthians 15:12-14
[98] 1 Corinthians 15:35
[99] Ezekiel 37:3
[100] 1 Corinthians 15:36
[101] Luke 11:40
[102] John 12:24
[103] 1 Corinthians 15:37

"But God gives it a body as he has determined, and to each kind of seed he gives its own body."[104]

"Then God said, let the land produce vegetation: seed-bearing plants and trees on the land that bear fruit with seed in it, according to their various kinds. And it was so."[105]

"Not all flesh is the same: People have one kind of flesh, animals have another, birds another and fish another."[106]

"There are also heavenly bodies and there are earthly bodies; but the splendor of the heavenly bodies is one kind, and the splendor of the earthly bodies is another."[107]

"The sun has one kind of splendor, the moon another and the stars another; and star differs from star in splendor."[108]

"So, will it be with the resurrection of the dead. The body that is sown is perishable, it is raised imperishable;"[109]

"Those who are wise will shine like the brightness of the heavens, and those who lead many to righteousness, like the stars for ever and ever."[110]

"Then the righteous will shine like the sun in the kingdom of their Father. Whoever has ears, let them hear."[111]

"It is sown in dishonor, it is raised in glory, it is sown in weakness, it is raised in power."[112]

"Who by the power that enables him to bring everything under his control will transform our lowly bodies so that they will be like his glorious body."[113]

"When Christ who is your life appears, then you also will appear with him in glory."[114]

---

[104] 1 Corinthians 15:38
[105] Genesis 1:11
[106] 1 Corinthians 15:39
[107] 1 Corinthians 15:40
[108] 1 Corinthians 15:41
[109] 1 Corinthians 15:42
[110] Daniel 12:3
[111] Matthew 13:43
[112] 1 Corinthians 15:43
[113] Philippians 3:21
[114] Colossians 3:4

"It is sown in a natural body it is raised a spiritual body. If there is a natural body, there is also a spiritual body."[115]

"The first man Adam became a living being, the last Adam, a life-giving spirit."[116]

"Then the LORD God formed a man from the dust of the ground and breathed into his nostrils the breath of life, and the man became a living being."[117]

"For just as the Father raises the dead and gives them life, even so the Son gives life to whom he is pleased to give it."[118]

"Because through Christ Jesus the law of the Spirit who gives life has set you free from the law of sin and death."[119]

"The first man was of the dust of the earth; the second man is of heaven."[120]

"No one has ever gone into heaven except the one who came from heaven the Son of Man."[121]

"The one who comes from above is above all; the one who is from the earth belongs to the earth and speaks as one from the earth. The one who comes from heaven is above all."[122]

"As was the earthly man, so are those who are of the earth; and as is the heavenly man, so also are those who are of heaven."[123]

"But our citizenship is in heaven. And we eagerly await a Savior from there, the Lord Jesus Christ."[124]

"And just as we have borne the image of the earthly man, so shall we bear the image of the heavenly man."[125]

---

[115] 1 Corinthians 15:44
[116] 1 Corinthians 15:45
[117] Genesis 2:7
[118] John 5:21
[119] Romans 8:2
[120] 1 Corinthians 15:47
[121] John 3:13
[122] John 3:31
[123] 1 Corinthians 15:48
[124] Philippians 3:20
[125] 1 Corinthians 15:49

"For those God foreknew he also predestined to be conformed to the image of his Son, that he might be the firstborn among many brothers and sisters."[126]

"I declare to you, brothers and sisters, that flesh and blood cannot inherit the kingdom of God, nor does the perishable inherit the imperishable."[127]

"Jesus replied, Very, truly I tell you, no one can see the kingdom of God unless they are born again."[128]

"Jesus answered, 'Very, truly I tell you, no one can enter the kingdom of God unless they are born of water and the Spirit'."[129]

"For we know that if the earthly tent we live in is destroyed, we have a building from God, an eternal house in heaven, not built by human hands."[130]

"Do you not know that your bodies are temples of the Holy Spirit, who is in you, whom you have received from God? You are not your own;"[131]

"You were brought at a price. Therefore, honor God with your bodies."[132]

"Yet to all who did receive him, to those who believed in his name, he gave the right to become children of God."[133]

"Children born not of natural descent, nor of human decision or a husband's will, but born of God."[134]

"Now the one who has fashioned us for this very purpose is God, who has given us the Spirit as a deposit, guaranteeing what is to come."[135]

---

[126] Romans 8:29
[127] 1 Corinthians 15:50
[128] John 3:3
[129] John 3:5
[130] 2 Corinthians 5:1
[131] 1 Corinthians 6:19
[132] 1 Corinthians 6:20
[133] John 1:12
[134] John 1:13
[135] 2 Corinthians 5:5

"Now it is God who makes both us and you stand firm in Christ. He anointed us."[136]

"Set his seal of ownership on us and put his Spirit in our hearts as a deposit, guaranteeing what is to come."[137]

"Therefore, long as we are at home in the body we are away from the Lord."[138]

"For we live by faith, not by sight."[139]

---

[136] 2 Corinthians 1:21
[137] 2 Corinthians 1:22
[138] 2 Corinthians 5:6
[139] 2 Corinthians 5:7

THE
FATHER'S
LOVE
FOR
HIS
LOST
SON

For this son of mine was dead and is alive again; he was lost and is found so they began to celebrate.

The Father's Love for His Lost Son

(Luke 15:11–32)

There was a man who had two sons. The younger one said to his father, Father, give me my share of the estate. He divided his property between them. Not long after that, the younger son got together all he had, set off for a distant country and there squandered his wealth in wild living. After he had spent everything, there was a severe famine in that whole country, and he began to be in need. He went and hired himself out to a citizen of that country, who sent him to his fields to feed pigs. He longed to fill his stomach with the pods that the pigs were eating, but no one give him anything. When he came to his senses, he said, how many of my father's hired servants have food to spare, and here I am starving to death! I will set out and go back to my father and say to him: Father, I have sinned against heaven and against you. I am no longer worthy to be called your son; make me like one of your hired servants. He got up and went to his father. But while he was still a long way off, his father saw him and was filled with compassion for him; he ran to his son, threw his arms around him and kissed him. The son said to him, Father, I have sinned against heaven and against you. I am no longer worthy to be called your son. But the father said to his servants, Quick! Bring the best robe and put it on him. Put a ring on his finger and sandals on his feet. Bring the fattened calf and kill it let us have a feast and celebrate. For this son of mine was dead and is alive again; he was lost and is found so they began to celebrate. Meanwhile, the older son was in the field. When he came near the house, he heard music and dancing. He called one of the servants and asked him what was going on. Your brother has come, he replied, and your father has killed the fattened calf because he has him back safe and sound. The older brother became angry and refused to go in. The father went out and pleaded with him. But he answered his father, Look! All these years I have been slaving for you and never disobeyed your orders. Yet you never gave me even a young goat so I could celebrate with my friends. But when this son of yours who has squandered your property with prostitutes comes home, you kill the fattened calf for him! My son, the father said, you are always with me, and everything I have is yours. But we had to celebrate and be glad, because this brother of yours was dead and is alive again; he was lost and is found.

I love this story because it demonstrated what this book is all about—the Father's love is unconditional. When the son return home to his father, not one time did the father said anything about how his son had wasted his wealth or tell him how he was wrong. No, he was filled with compassion for his son, ran to him, and threw his arms around his son and kissed him. While the son was telling the father how sorry he was for what he has done, did you notice that the father never responded to what his son was saying? When I read this story, I see how much the father loves his sons, and that is how much God our Father loves us. I also see in this story how the older son was angry with his father for showing love and compassion for his younger brother. Instead of the older son being happy that his brother was home safe, no, he believed that because he never disobeyed his father, he should be the one celebrated. That is the way some people believe that God our Father should bless them because of how much good works they do. But our Father is not like that. His arms are always opened wide for his lost children who return to him. Our Father God looks at the heart; make sure what you are doing comes from a pure heart because we were created to love and were blessed to be a blessing. The Father God said to us just like the older son, the father said to him, "Son, you are always with me and all that I have is yours, but you never ask me." Ask and it will be given to you, for everyone who asks receives. The Father loves for his children; he cares for his lost sheep.

THE
FATHER
GOD
IS
LOVE

Whoever does not love does not know God, because God is love.

—1 John 4:8

The Father God Is Love

"Dear friends, let us love one another, for love comes from God. Everyone who loves has been born of God and knows God" (1 John 4:7).

"For this is the message you heard from the beginning: We should love one another" (1 John 3:11).

"Whoever says, I know him, but does not do what He commands is a liar, and the truth is not in that person" (1 John 2:4).

"Whoever does not love does not know God, because God is love" (1 John 4:8).

"This is how God showed his love among us: He sent his one and only Son into the world that we might live through him" (1 John 4:9).

"For God so loved the world that he gave his one and only Son, that whoever believes in him shall not perish but have eternal life" (John 3:16).

"For God did not send his Son into the world to condemn the world, but to save the world through him" (John 3:17).

"And this is the testimony: God has given us eternal life, and this life is in his Son" (1 John 5:11).

"This is love: not that we loved God, but that he loved us and sent his Son as an atoning sacrifice for our sins" (1 John 4:10).

"But God demonstrates his own love for us in this: While we were still sinners, Christ died for us" (Romans 5:8).

"For if, while we were God's enemies, we were reconciled to him through the death of his Son, how much more, having been reconciled, shall we be saved through his life!" (Romans 5:10).

"He is the atoning sacrifice for our sins, and not only for ours but also for the sins of the whole world" (1 John 2:2).

"Dear friends, since God so loved us, we also ought to love one another" (1 John 4:11).

"No one has ever seen God; but if we love one another, God lives in us and his love is made complete in us" (1 John 4:12).

"No one has ever seen God, but the one and only Son, who is himself God and is in closest relationship with the Father, has made him know" (John 1:18).

"But if anyone obeys his word, love for God is truly made complete in them. This is how we know we are in him" (1 John 2:5).

"This is how we know that we live in him and he in us: He has given us of his Spirit" (1 John 4:13).

"And we have seen and testify, that the Father has sent his Son to be the Savior of the world" (1 John 4:14).

"And you also must testify, for you have been with me from the beginning" (John 15:27).

"If anyone acknowledges that Jesus is the Son of God, God lives in them and they are in God" (1 John 4:15).

"If you declare with your mouth, Jesus is Lord, and believe in your heart that God raised him from the dead, you will be saved" (Romans 10:9).

"And so we know and rely on the love God has for us. God is love. Whoever lives in love lives in God, and God in them" (1 John 4:16).

"This is how love is made complete among us so that we will have confidence on the day of judgment: In this world we are like Jesus" (1 John 4:17).

"There is no fear in love. But perfect love drives out fear because fear has to do with punishment. The one who fears is not made perfect in love" (1 John 4:18).

"The Spirit you received does not make you slaves, so that you live in fear again, rather, the Spirit you received brought about your adoption to sonship. And by him we cry Abba, Father" (Romans 8:15).

"Whoever claims to love God yet hates a brother or sister is a liar. For whoever does not love their brother or sister, whom they have seen, cannot love God, whom they have not seen" (1 John 4:20).

"And he has given us this command: Anyone who loves God must also love their brother or sister" (1 John 4:21).

"We love because he first loved us" (1 John 4:19).

THE
Father
Lovingly
Adopts
Us

He predestined us for adoption to sonship through Jesus Christ, in accordance with his pleasure and will.

—Ephesians 1:5

The Father Lovingly Adopts Us

"Praise be to the God and Father of our Lord Jesus Christ, who has blessed us in the heavenly realms with every spiritual blessing in Christ" (Ephesians 1:3).

"Praise be to the God and Father of our Lord Jesus Christ, the Father of compassion and the God of all comfort" (2 Corinthians 1:3).

"His intent was that now, through the church, the manifold wisdom of God should be made known to the rulers and authorities in the heavenly realms" (Ephesians 3:10).

"For he chose us in him before the creation of the world to be holy and blameless in his sight. In love" (Ephesians 1:4).

"And to present her to himself as a radiant church, without stain or wrinkle or any other blemish, but holy and blameless" (Ephesians 5:27).

"But now he has reconciled you by Christ's physical body through death to present you holy in his sight, without blemish and free from accusation" (Colossians 1:22).

"Be completely humble and gentle; be patient, bearing with one another in love" (Ephesians 4:2).

"Instead, speaking the truth in love, we will grow to become in every respect the mature body of him who is the head, that is, Christ" (Ephesians 4:15).

"From him the whole body, joined and held together by every supporting ligament, grows and builds itself up in love, as each part does its work" (Ephesians 4:16).

"He predestined us for adoption to sonship through Jesus Christ, in accordance with his pleasure and will" (Ephesians 1:5)

"For those God fore-knew he also predestined to be conformed to the image of his Son, that he might be the firstborn among many brothers and sisters" (Romans 8:29).

"And those he predestined, he also called; those he called, he also justified; those he justified, he also glorified" (Romans 8:30).

"For since in the wisdom of God the world through its wisdom did not know him, God was pleased through the foolishness of what was preached to save those who believe" (1 Corinthians 1:21).

"To the praise of his glorious grace, which he has freely given us in the One he love" (Ephesians 1:6).

"And a voice from heaven said, this is my Son, whom I love; with him I am well pleased" (Matthew 3:17).

"In him we have redemption through his blood, the forgiveness of sins, in accordance with the riches of God's grace" (Ephesians 1:7).

"And all are justified freely by his grace through the redemption that came by Christ Jesus" (Romans 3:24).

"That he lavished on us. With all wisdom and understanding" (Ephesians 1:8).

"He made known to us the mystery of his will according to his good pleasure, which he purposed in Christ" (Ephesians 1:9).

"To be put into effect when the times reach their fulfillment to bring unity to all things in heaven and on earth under Christ" (Ephesians 1:10).

"But when the set time had fully come, God sent his Son, born of a woman, born under the law" (Galatians 4:4).

And through him to reconcile to himself all things, whether things on earth or things in heaven, by making peace through his blood, shed on the cross" (Colossians 1:20).

"In him we were also chosen, having been predestined according to the plan of him who works out everything in conformity with the purpose of his will" (Ephesians 1:11).

"According to his eternal purpose that he accomplished in Christ Jesus our Lord" (Ephesians 3:11).

"Because God wanted to make the unchanging nature of his purpose very clear to the heirs of what was promised, he confirmed it with an oath" (Hebrews 6:17).

"In order that we, who were the first to put our hope in Christ, might be for the praise of his glory" (Ephesians 1:12).

"And you also were included in Christ when you heard the message of truth, the gospel of your salvation. When you believed, you were marked in him with a seal, the promised Holy Spirit" (Ephesians 1:13).

"The faith and love that spring from the hope stored up for you in heaven and about which you have already heard in the true message of the gospel" (Colossians 1:5).

"See what great love the Father has lavished on us, that we should be called children of God!" (1 John 3:1).

THE
FATHER
LOVES
US
DESPITE
OUR
SINFUL
NATURE

For it is by grace you have been saved, through faith
and this is not of yourselves, it is the gift of God.

—Ephesians 2:8

The Father Loves Us Despite Our Sinful Nature

"As for you, you were dead in your transgressions and sins" (Ephesians 2:1).

"But because of his great love for us, God, who is rich in mercy made us alive with Christ even when we were dead in transgressions it is by grace you have been saved" (Ephesians 2:4–5).

"When you were dead in your sins and in the uncircumcision of your flesh, God made you alive with Christ. He forgave us all our sins" (Colossians 2:13).

"In which you used to live when you followed the ways of this world and of the ruler of the kingdom of the air, the spirit who is now at work in those who are disobedient" (Ephesians 2:2).

"You used to walk in these ways, in the life you once lived" (Colossians 3:7).

"For our struggle is not against flesh and blood, but against the rulers, against the authorities, against the powers of this dark world and against the spiritual forces of evil in the heavenly realms" (Ephesians 6:12).

"Let no one deceive you with empty words, for because of such things God's wrath comes on those who are disobedient" (Ephesians 5:6).

"All of us also lived among them at one time, gratifying the cravings of our flesh and following its desires and thoughts. Like the rest, we were by nature deserving of wrath" Ephesians 2:3).

"So I say, walk by the Spirit, and you will not gratify the desires of the flesh" (Galatians 5:16).

"And God raised us up with Christ and seated us with him in the heavenly realms in Christ Jesus" (Ephesians 2:6).

"For it is by grace you have been saved, through faith and this is not from yourselves, it is the gift of God" (Ephesians 2:8).

"Not by works, so that no one can boast" (Ephesians 2:9).

He has saved us and called us to a holy life not because of anything we have done but because of his own purpose and grace. This grace was given us in Christ Jesus before the beginning of time" (2 Timothy 1:9).

"So that no one may boast before him" (1 Corinthians 1:29).

"For we are God's handiwork, created in Christ Jesus to do good works, which God prepared in advance for us to do" (Ephesians 2:10).

"And to put on the new self, created to be like God in true righteousness and holiness" (Ephesians 4:24).

"Who gave himself for us to redeem us from all wickedness and to purify for himself a people that are his very own, eager to do what is good" (Titus 2:14).

Freedom in Christ's Love

It is for freedom that Christ has set us free.

—Galatians 5:1

Freedom in Christ's Love

"It is for freedom that Christ has set us free. Stand firm, then, and do not let yourselves be burdened again by a yoke of slavery" (Galatians 5:1).

"Then you will know the truth, and the truth will set you free" (John 8:32).

"Be on your guard; stand firm in the faith; be courageous; be strong" (1 Corinthians 16:13)

"This matter arose because some false believers had infiltrated our ranks to spy on the freedom we have in Christ Jesus and to make us slaves" (Galatians 2:4).

"Mark my words! I, Paul, tell you that if you let yourselves be circumcised, Christ will be of no value to you at all" (Galatians 5:2).

"Certain people came down from Judea to Antioch and were teaching the believers: unless you are circumcised, according to the custom taught by Moses, you cannot be saved" (Acts 15:1).

"Again I declare to every man who lets himself be Circumcised that he is obligated to obey the whole law" (Galatians 5:3).

"For all who rely on the works of the law are under a curse, as it is written cursed is everyone who does not continue to do everything written in the Book of the Law" (Galatians 3:10).

"You who are trying to be justified by the law have been alienated from Christ; you have fallen away from grace" (Galatians 5:4)

"See to it that no one falls short of the grace of God and that no bitter root grows up to cause trouble and defile many" (Hebrews 12:15).

"For it is better if it is God's will, to suffer for doing good than for doing evil" (1 Peter 3:17).

"For through the Spirit we eagerly await by faith the righteousness for which we hope" (Galatians 5:5).

"Not only so, but we ourselves, who have the first fruits of the Spirit, groan inwardly as we wait eagerly for our adoption to sonship, the redemption of our bodies" (Romans 8:23).

"For in this hope we were saved. But hope that is seen is no hope at all. Who hopes for what they already have?" (Romans 8:24).

"For in Christ Jesus neither circumcision nor uncircumcision has any value. The only thing that counts is faith expressing itself through love" (Galatians 5:6).

"We remember before our God and Father your work produced by faith, your labor prompted by love, and your endurance inspired by hope in our Lord Jesus Christ" (1 Thessalonians 1:3).

"You were running a good race. Who cut in on you to keep you from obeying the truth?" (Galatians 5:7).

"Do you not know that in a race all the runners run, but only one gets the prize? Run in such a way as to get the prize" (1 Corinthians 9:24).

"You foolish Galatians! Who has bewitched you? Before your very eyes Jesus Christ was clearly portrayed as crucified" (Galatians 3:1).

"That kind of persuasion does not come from the one who calls you" (Galatians 5:8).

"And we know that in all things God works for the good of those who love him, who have been called according to his purpose" (Romans 8:28).

"I am astonished that you are so quickly deserting the one who called you to live in the grace of Christ and are turning to a different gospel" (Galatians 1:6).

"Which is really no gospel at all. Evidently some people are throwing you into confusion and are trying to pervert the gospel of Christ" (Galatians 1:7).

"I am confident in the Lord that you will take no other view. The one who is throwing you into confusion, whoever that may be, will have to pay the penalty" (Galatians 5:10)

"All of us, then, who are mature should take such a view of things and if on some point you think differently, that too God will make clear to you" (Philippians 3:15).

"You, my brothers and sisters, were called to be free. But do not use your freedom to indulge the flesh, rather, serve one another humbly in love" (Galatians 5:13).

"Be careful, however, that the exercise of your rights does not become a stumbling block to the weak" (1 Corinthians 8:9).

"Live as free people, but do not use your freedom as a cover up for evil; live as God's slaves" (1 Peter 2:16).

"Submit to one another out of reverence for Christ" (Ephesians 5:21).

"For the entire law is fulfilled in keeping this one command: Love your neighbor as yourself" (Galatians 5:14).

"If you bite and devour each other, watch out or you will be destroyed by each other" (Galatians 5:15).

"So if the Son sets you free, you will be free indeed" (John 8:36).

YOUR
LIFE
IS
NOW
HIDDEN
WITH
CHRIST
IN
THE
FATHER

For you died, and your life is now hidden with Christ in God.

—Colossians 3:3

Your Life Is Now Hidden with Christ in the Father

"The Son is the image of the invisible God, the firstborn over all creation" (Colossians 1:15).

"The god of this age has blinded the minds of unbelievers, so that they cannot see the light of the gospel that displays the glory of Christ, who is the image of God" (2 Corinthians 4:4).

"No one has ever seen God, but the one and only Son, who is himself God and is in closest relationship with the Father, has made him know" (John 1:18).

"For in him all things were created: things in heaven and on earth, visible and invisible, whether thrones or powers or rulers or authorities; all things have been created through him and for him" (Colossians 1:16).

"Through him all things were made; without him nothing was made that has been made" (John 1:3).

"He exerted when he raised Christ from the dead and seated him at his right hand in the heavenly realms" (Ephesians 1:20).

"Far above all rule and authority, power and dominion, and every name that is invoked, not only in the present age but also in the one to come" (Ephesians 1:21).

"He is before all things, and in him all things hold together" (Colossians 1:17).

"He was with God in the beginning" (John 1:2).

"And he is the head of the body, the church; he is the beginning and the firstborn from among the dead, so that in everything he might have the supremacy" (Colossians 1:18).

"And God placed all things under his feet and appointed him to be head over everything for the church" (Ephesians 1:22).

"That the Messiah would suffer and, as the first to rise from the dead, would bring the message of light to his own people and to the Gentiles" (Acts 26:23).

and from Jesus Christ, who is the faithful witness, the firstborn from the dead, and the ruler of the kings of the earth. To him who loves us and has freed us from our sins by his blood" (Revelation 1:5).

"For God was pleased to have all his fullness dwell in him" (Colossians 1:19)

"He predestined us for adoption to sonship through Jesus Christ, in accordance with his pleasure and will" (Ephesians 1:5).

"Out of his fullness we have all received grace in place of grace already given" (John 1:16).

"And through him to reconcile to himself all things, whether things on earth or things in heaven, by making peace through his blood, shed on the cross" (Colossians 1:20)

"All is from God, who reconciled us to himself through Christ and gave us the ministry of reconciliation" (2 Corinthians 5:18).

"To be put into effect when the times reach their fulfillment to bring unity to all things in heaven and on earth under Christ" (Ephesians 1:10).

"But now in Christ Jesus you who once were far away have been brought near by the blood of Christ" (Ephesians 2:13).

"Once you were alienated from God and were enemies in your minds because of your evil behavior" (Colossians 1:21)

"For if, while we were God's enemies, we were reconciled to him through the death of his Son, how much more, having been reconciled, shall we be saved through his life!" (Romans 5:10).

"All of us also lived among them at one time, gratifying the cravings of our flesh and following its desires and thoughts. Like the rest, we were by nature deserving of wrath" (Ephesians 2:3).

"But now he has reconciled you by Christ's physical body through death to present you holy in his sight, without blemish and free from accusation" (Colossians 1:22).

"So, my brothers and sisters, you also died to the law through the body of Christ, that you might belong to another, to him who was raised from the dead, in order that we might bear fruit for God" (Romans 7:4).

"And to present her to himself as a radiant church, without stain or wrinkle or any other blemish, but holy and blameless" (Ephesians 5:27).

"So that Christ may dwell in your hearts through faith. And I pray that you, being rooted and established in love" (Ephesians 3:17).

"The faith and love that spring from the hope stored up for you in heaven and about which you have already heard in the true message of the gospel" (Colossians 1:5).

"I have become its servant by the commission God gave me to present to you the word of God in its fullness" (Colossians 1:25).

"To them God has chosen to make known among the Gentiles the glorious riches of this mystery, which is Christ in you, the hope of glory" (Colossians 1:27).

"He is the one we proclaim, admonishing and teaching everyone with all wisdom, so that we may present everyone fully mature in Christ" (Colossians 1:28).

"Since then, you have been raised with Christ, set your hearts on things above, where Christ is, seated at the right hand of God" (Colossians 3:1).

"Set your minds on things above, not on earthly things" (Colossians 3:2).

"For you died, and your life is now hidden with Christ in God" (Colossians 3:3).

CHRISTIANS
SHOULD
NOT
LOVE
THE
WORLD

If anyone loves the world, love for the Father is not in them.

—1 John 2:15

Christians Should Not Love the World

"Do not love the world or anything in the world. If anyone loves the world, love for the Father is not in them" (1 John 2:15).

"Do not conform to the pattern of this world but be transformed by the renewing of your mind. Then you will be able to test and approve what God's will is, his good pleasing and perfect will" (Romans 12:2).

"You adulterous people, don't you know that friendship with the world means enmity against God? Therefore, anyone who chooses to be a friend of the world becomes an enemy of God" (James 4:4).

"For everything in the world the lust of the flesh, the lust of the eyes, and the pride of life comes not from the Father but from the world" (1 John 2:16).

"Rather, clothe yourselves with the Lord Jesus Christ, and do not think about how to gratify the desires of the flesh" (Romans 13:14).

"Death and Destruction are never satisfied, and neither are human eyes" (Proverbs 27:20).

"Submit yourselves, then to God. Resist the devil, and he will flee from you" (James 4:7).

"Come near to God and he will come near to you. Wash your hands, you sinners, and purify your hearts, you double-minded" (James 4:8).

"Humble yourselves before the Lord, and he will lift you up" (James 4:10).

"Peace I leave with you; my peace I give you. I do not give to you as the world gives. Do not let your hearts be troubled and do not be afraid" (John 14:27).

"I have told you these things, so that in me you may have peace. In this world you will have trouble. But take heart! I have overcome the world" (John 16:33).

"The world and its desires pass away, but whoever does the will of God lives forever" (1 John 2:17).

TEMPTATIONS
ARE
NOT
FROM
GOD
THE
FATHER

When tempted no one should say, God is tempting me. For God cannot be tempted by evil, nor does he tempt anyone.

—James 1:13

Temptations Are Not from God the Father

"Consider it pure joy, my brothers and sisters, whenever you face trials of many kinds" (James 1:2).

"Because you know that the testing of your faith produces perseverance" (James 1:3).

"Let perseverance finish its work so that you may be mature and complete, not lacking anything" (James 1:4).

"If any of you lacks wisdom, you should ask God, who gives generously to all without finding fault, and it will be given to you" (James 1:5).

"For the Lord gives wisdom; from his mouth come knowledge and understanding" (Proverbs 2:6).

"Ask and it will be given to you; seek and you will find; knock and the door will be opened to you" (Matthew 7:7).

"But when you ask, you must believe and not doubt, because the one doubts is like a wave of the sea, blown and tossed by the wind" (James 1:6).

"Therefore I tell you, whatever you ask for in prayer, believe that you have received it, and it will be yours" (Mark 11:24).

"Come near to God and he will come near to you. Wash your hands, you sinners, and purify your hearts, you double-minded" (James 4:8).

"Those who use the things of the world, as if not engrossed in them. For this world in its present form is passing away" (1 Corinthians 7:31).

"Blessed is the one who perseveres under trial because, having stood the test, that person will receive the crown of life that the Lord has promised to those who love him" (James 1:12).

"Everyone who competes in the games goes into strict training. They do it to get a crown that will not last, but we do it to get a crown that will last forever" (1 Corinthians 9:25).

"Listen, my dear brothers and sisters: Has not God chosen those who are poor in the eyes of the world to be rich in faith and to inherit the kingdom he promised those who love him?" (James 2:5).

"When tempted, no one should say, God is tempting me. For God cannot be tempted by evil, nor does he tempt anyone" (James 1:13).

"But each person is tempted when they are dragged away by their own evil desire and enticed" (James 1:14).

"Then, after desire has conceived, it gives birth to sin, and sin, when it is full-grown, gives birth to death" (James 1:15).

"Whoever is pregnant with evil conceives trouble and gives birth to disillusionment" (Psalm 7:14).

"For the wages of sin is death, but the gift of God is eternal life in Christ Jesus our Lord" (Romans 6:23).

"Do you not know that wrongdoers will not inherit the kingdom of God? Do not be deceived: Neither the sexually immoral nor idolaters nor adulterers nor men who have sex with men" (1 Corinthians 6:9).

"Nor thieves nor the greedy, nor drunkards nor slanderers nor swindlers will inherit the kingdom of God" (1 Corinthians 6:10).

"Every good and perfect gift is from above, coming down from the Father of the heavenly lights, who does not change like shifting shadows" (James 1:17).

"God is not human, that he should lie, not a human being, that he should change his mind. Does he speak and then not act? Does he promise and not fulfill?" (Numbers 23:19).

"He chose to give us birth through the word of truth, that we might be a kind of first fruits of all he created" (James 1:18).

"Child born not of natural descent, nor of human decision or a husband's will, but born of God" (John 1:13).

"In order that we, who were the first to put our hope in Christ, might be for the praise of his glory" (Ephesians 1:12).

"Sin is not ended by multiplying words but the prudent hold their tongues" (Proverbs 10:19).

"My dear brothers and sisters, take note of this: Everyone should be quick to listen, slow to speak and slow to become angry" (James 1:19).

"Because human anger does not produce the righteousness that God desires" (James 1:20).

"Therefore, get rid of all moral filth and the evil that is so prevalent and humbly accept the word planted in you, which can save you" (James 1:21).

"And you also were included in Christ when you heard the message of truth, the gospel of your salvation. When you believed, you were marked in him with a seal, the promised Holy Spirit" (Ephesians 1:13).

"Do not merely listens to the word, and so deceive yourselves. Do what it says" (James 1:22).

"Anyone who listens to the word but does not do what it says is like someone who looks at his face in a mirror" (James 1:23).

"And, after looking at himself, goes away and immediately forgets what he looks like" (James 1:24).

"But whoever looks intently into the perfect law that gives freedom and continues in it not forgetting what they have heard but doing it they will be blessed in what they do" (James 1:25).

"Speak and act as those who are going to be judged by the law that gives freedom" (James 2:12).

"Those who consider themselves religious and yet do not keep a tight rein on their tongues deceives themselves, and their religion is worthless" (James 1:26).

"Religion that God our Father accepts as pure faultless is this: to look after orphans and widows in their distress and to keep oneself from being polluted by the world" (James 1:27).

"Keep your tongue from evil and your lips from telling lies" (Psalm 34:13).

"For whoever would love life and see good days must keep their tongue from evil and their lips from deceitful speech" (1 Peter 3:10).

"No temptation has overtaken you except what is common to mankind. And God is faithful; he will not let you be tempted beyond what you can bear. But when you are tempted, he will also provide away out so that you can endure it" (1 Corinthians 10:13).

PUT
TO
DEATH
THE
EARTHLY
NATURE
AND
PUT
ON
LOVE

Put to death, therefore, whatever belongs to your
earthy nature: sexual immorality, impurity, lust,
evil desires and greed, which is idolatry.

—Colossians 3:5

Put to Death the Earthly Nature and Put on Love

"So I tell you this, and insist on it in the Lord, that you must no longer live as the Gentiles do, in the futility of their thinking" (Ephesians 4:17).

"For although they knew God, they neither glorified him as God nor gave thanks to him, but their thinking became futile and their foolish hearts were darkened" (Romans 1:21).

"They are darkened in their understanding and separated from the life of God because of the ignorance that is in them due to the hardening of their hearts" (Ephesians 4:18).

"Remember that all that time you were separate from Christ, excluded from citizenship in Israel and foreigners to the covenants of the promise, without hope and without God in the world" (Ephesians 2:12).

"But their minds were made dull, for to this day the same veil remains when the old covenant is read. It has not been removed, because only in Christ is it taken away" (2 Corinthians 3:14).

"Having lost all sensitivity, they have given themselves over to sensuality as to indulge in every kind of impurity, and they are full of greed" (Ephesians 4:19).

"For of this you can be sure: No immoral, impure or greedy person such a person is an idolater has any inheritance in the kingdom of Christ and of God" (Ephesians 5:5).

"Put to death, therefore, whatever belongs to your earthly nature: sexual immorality, impurity, lust, evil desires and greed, which is idolatry" (Colossians 3:5).

"But now you must also rid yourselves of all such things as these: anger, rage, malice, slander, and filthy language from your lips" (Colossians 3:8).

"Do not let any unwholesome talk come out of your mouths, but only what is helpful for building others up according to their needs, that it may benefit those who listen" (Ephesians 4:29).

"Because of these, the wrath of God is coming" (Colossians 3:6).

"Such teachings come through hypocritical liars, whose consciences have been seared as with a hot iron" (1 Timothy 4:2).

"You were taught with regard to your former way of life, to put off your old self, which is being corrupted by its deceitful desires" (Ephesians 4:22).

"Therefore each of you must put off falsehood and speak truthfully to your neighbor, for we are all members of one body" (Ephesians 4:25).

"For we know that our old self was crucified with him so that the body ruled by sin might be done away with, that we should no longer be slaves to sin" (Romans 6:6).

"We were therefore buried with him through baptism into death in order that, just as Christ was raised from the dead through the glory of the Father, we too may live a new life" (Romans 6:4).

"And to put on the new self, created to be like God in true righteousness and holiness" (Ephesians 4:24).

"For we are God's handiwork, created in Christ Jesus to do good works, which God prepared in advance for us to do" (Ephesians 2:10).

"So in Christ we, though many, form one body, and each member belongs to all the others" (Romans 12:5).

"Anyone who has been stealing must steal no longer, but must work, doing something useful with their own hands, that they may have something to share with those in need" (Ephesians 4:28).

"In everything I did, I showed you that by this kind of hard work we must help the weak, remembering, the words the Lord Jesus himself said: It is more blessed to give than to receive" (Acts 20:35).

"And to make it your ambition to lead a quiet life: you should mind your own business and work with your hands, just as we told you" (1 Thessalonians 4:11).

"Do nothing out of selfish ambition or vain conceit. Rather, in humility value others above yourselves" (Philippians 2:3).

"Bear with each other and forgive one another if any of you has a grievance against someone. Forgive as the Lord forgave you" (Colossians 3:13).

"Be kind and compassionate to one another, forgiving each other, just as in Christ God forgave you" (Ephesians 4:32).

"There is neither Jew nor Gentile, neither slave nor free, nor is there male and female, for you are all one in Christ Jesus" (Galatians 3:28).

"Therefore, as God's chosen people, holy and dearly loved, clothe yourselves with compassion, kindness, humility, gentleness and patience" (Colossians 3:12).

"And over all these virtues put on love, which binds them all together in perfect unity" (Colossians 3:14).

"In purity, understanding, patience and kindness; in the Holy Spirit and in sincere love" (2 Corinthians 6:6).

"Peace I leave with you; my peace I give you. I do not give to you as the world gives. Do not let your hearts be troubled and do not be afraid" (John 14:27).

"Let the peace of Christ rule in your hearts, since as members of one body you were called to peace and be thankful" (Colossians 3:15).

CHILDREN
OF
GOD'S
LOVE
SHOULD
SHINE
LIKE
STARS

For you were once darkness, but now you are
light in the Lord. Live as children of light.

—Ephesians 5:8

Children of God's Love Should Shine Like Stars

"Follow God's example, therefore, as dearly loved children" (Ephesians 5:1).

"And walk in the way of love, just as Christ loved us and gave himself up for us as a fragrant offering and sacrifice to God" (Ephesians 5:2).

"For we are to God the pleasing aroma of Christ among those who are being saved and those who are perishing" (2 Corinthians 2:15).

"Who give himself for our sins to rescue us from the present evil age, according to the will of our God and Father" (Galatians 1:4).

"Unlike the other high priests, he does not need to offer sacrifices day after day, first for his own sins, and then the sins of the people. He sacrificed for their sins once for all when he offered himself" (Hebrews 7:27).

"But among you there must not be even a hint of sexual immorality, or of any kind of impunity, or of greed, because these are improper for God's holy people" (Ephesians 5:3).

"Nor should there be obscenity, foolish talk or coarse joking, which are out of place, but rather thanksgiving" (Ephesians 5:4).

"Let no one deceive you with empty words, for because of such things God's wrath comes on those who are disobedient" (Ephesians 5:6).

"The wrath of God is being revealed from heaven against all the godlessness and wickedness of people, who suppress the truth by their wickedness" (Romans 1:18).

"In which you used to live when you followed the ways of this world and of the ruler of the kingdom of the air, the spirit who is now at work in those who are disobedient" (Ephesians 2:2).

"That you may be children of your Father in heaven. He causes his sun to rise on the evil and the good and sends rain on the righteous and the unrighteous" (Matthew 5:45).

"For you were once darkness, but now your light in the Lord. Live as children of light" (Ephesians 5:8).

"For the fruit of the light consists in all goodness, righteousness and truth" (Ephesians 5:9).

"But everything exposed by the light becomes visible and everything that is illuminated becomes a light" (Ephesians 5:13).

"Everyone who does evil hates the light and will not come into the light for fear that their deeds will be exposed" (John 3:20).

"But whoever lives by the truth comes into the light, so that it may be seen plainly that what they have done has been done in the sight of God" (John 3:21).

"Be very careful, then, how you live not as unwise but as wise" (Ephesians 5:15).

"Making the most of every opportunity, because the days are evil" (Ephesians 5:16).

"Therefore do not be foolish but understand what the Lord's will is" (Ephesians 5:17).

"Therefore put on the full armor of God, so that when the day of evil comes, you may be able to stand your ground, and after you have done everything, to stand" (Ephesians 6:13).

"For it is God who works in you to will and to act in order to fulfill his good purpose" (Philippians 2:13).

"Arise, shine, for your light has come, and the glory of the LORD rises upon you" (Isaiah 60:1).

"You are all children of the light and children of the day. We do not belong to the night or to the darkness" (1 Thessalonians 5:5).

"You are the light of the world. A town built on a hill cannot be hidden" (Matthew 5:14).

"Submit to one another out of reverence for Christ" (Ephesians 5:21).

"So that you may become blameless and pure, children of God without fault in a warped and crooked generation. Then you will shine among them like stars in the sky" (Philippians 2:15).

"Those who are wise will shine like the brightness of the heavens, and those who lead many to righteousness, like the stars for ever and ever" (Daniel 12:3).

LOVE
ONE
ANOTHER

A new command I give you: Love one another. As I
have loved you, so you must love one another.

—John 13:34

Love One Another

"For this is the message you heard from the beginning: We should love one another" (1 John 3:11).

"This is the message we have heard from him and declare to you: God is light; in him there is no darkness at all" (1 John 1:5).

"Anyone who claims to be in the light but hates a brother or sister is still in the darkness" (1 John 2:9).

"By this everyone will know that you are my disciples, if you love one another" (John 13:35).

"Do not be surprised, my brothers and sisters, if the world hates you" (1 John 3:13).

"If you belonged to the world, it would love you as its own. As it is, you do not belong to the world, but I chose you out of the world; that is why the world hates you" (John 15:19).

"I have given them your word and the world has hated them, for they are not of the world any more than I am of the world" (John 17:14).

"We know that we have passed from death to life, because we love each other. Anyone who does not love remains in death" (1 John 3:14).

"Anyone who hates a brother or sister is a murderer, and you know that no murderer has eternal life residing in him" (1 John 3:15).

"You belong to your father, the devil, and you want to carry out your father's desires. He was a murderer from the beginning, not holding to the truth, for there is no truth in him. When he lies, he speaks his native language, for he is a liar and the father of lies" (John 8:44).

"Whoever claims to love God yet hates a brother or sister is a liar. For whoever does not love their brother and sister, whom they have seen, cannot love God, whom they have not seen" (1 John 4:20).

"If anyone has material possessions and sees a brother or sister in need but has no pity on them, how can the love of God be in that person?" (1 John 3:17).

"Share with the Lord's people who are in need. Practice hospitality" (Romans 12:13).

"Dear children, let us not love with words or speech but with actions and in truth" (1 John 3:18).

"My people come to you, as they usually do, and sit before you to hear your words, but they do not put them into practice. Their mouths speak of love, but their hearts are greedy for unjust gain" (Ezekiel 33:31).

"Love must be sincere. Hate what is evil; cling to what is good" (Romans 12:9).

"The goal of this command is love, which comes from a pure heart and a good conscience and a sincere faith" (1 Timothy 1:5).

"Be devoted to one another in love. Honor one another above yourselves" (Romans 12:10).

"Keep on loving one another as brothers and sisters" (Hebrews 13:1).

"Do nothing out of selfish ambition or vain conceit. Rather, in humility value others above yourselves" (Philippians 2:3).

"Bless those who persecute you; bless and do not curse" (Romans 12:14).

"But I tell you, love your enemies and pray for those who persecute you" (Matthew 5:44).

"Rejoice with those who rejoice; mourn with those who mourn" (Romans 12:15).

"Live in harmony with one another, do not be proud, but be willing to associate with people of low position. Do not be conceited" (Romans 12:16).

"May the God who gives endurance and encouragement give you the same, attitude of mind toward each other that Christ Jesus had" (Romans 15:5).

"Do not repay anyone evil for evil. Be careful to do what is right in the eyes of everyone" (Romans 12:17).

"Do not say, I will pay you back for this wrong! Wait for the LORD, and he will avenge you" (Proverbs 20:22).

"For we are taking pains to do what is right, not only in the eyes of the Lord but also in the eyes of men" (2 Corinthians 8:21).

"If it is possible, as far as it depends on you, live at peace with everyone" (Romans 12:18).

"Salt is good, but if it loses its saltiness, how can you make it salty again? Have salt among yourselves; and be at peace with each other" (Mark 9:50).

"Let us therefore make every effort to do what leads to peace and to mutual edification" (Romans 14:19).

"Do not take revenge, my dear friends, but leave room for God's wrath, for it is written: It is mine to avenge; I will repay, says the Lord" (Romans 12:19).

"On the contrary: If your enemy is hungry, feed him; if he is thirsty, give him something to drink" (Romans 12:20).

"Above all, love each other deeply, because love covers over a multitude of sins" (1 Peter 4:8).

"Do not be overcome by evil but overcome evil with good" (Romans 12:21).

"You need to persevere so that when you have done the will of God, you will receive what he has promised" (Hebrews 10:36).

"A new command I give you: Love one another. As I have loved you, so you must love one another" (John 13:34).

DEBT
OF
THE
FATHER'S
LOVE

Let no debt remain outstanding except the
continuing debt to love one another.

—Romans 13:8

Debt of the Father's Love

"Let no debt remain outstanding, except the continuing debt to love one another, for whoever loves others has fulfilled the law" (Romans 13:8).

"For the entire law is fulfilled in keeping this one command: Love your neighbor as yourself" (Galatians 5:14).

"The commandments, you shall not commit adultery, you shall not murder, you shall not steal, you shall not covet, and whatever other command there may be, are summed up in this one command: Love your neighbor as yourself" (Romans 13:9).

"Honor your father and mother and love your neighbor as yourself" (Matthew 19:19).

"Love does no harm to a neighbor Therefore love is the fulfillment of the law" (Romans 13:10).

"Gentleness and self-control. Against such things there is no law" (Galatians 5:23).

"This is why it is said wake up, sleeper, rise from the dead, and Christ will shine on you" (Ephesians 5:14).

"The night is nearly over; the day is almost here so let us put aside the deeds of darkness and put on the armor of light" (Romans 13:12).

"Those who belong to Christ Jesus have crucified the flesh with its passions and desires" (Galatians 5:24).

"For we know that our old self was crucified with him so that the body ruled by sin might be done away with, that we should no longer be slaves to sin" (Romans 6:6).

"Yet I am writing you a new command; its truth is seen in him and in you because the darkness is passing, and the true light is already shining" (1 John 2:8).

"Put on the full armor of God, so that you can take your stand against the devil's schemes" (Ephesians 6:11).

"Let us behave decently, as in the daytime, not in carousing and drunkenness, not in sexual immorality and debauchery, not in dissension and jealousy" (Romans 13:13).

"Idolatry and witchcraft; hatred, discord, jealously, fits of rage, selfish ambition, dissensions, factions" (Galatians 5:20).

"And envy; drunkenness, orgies, and the like. I warn you, as I did before, that those who live like this will not inherit the Kingdom of God" (Galatians 5:21).

"Rather, clothe yourselves with the Lord Jesus Christ, and do not think about how to gratify the desires of the flesh" (Romans 13:14).

"For all of you who were baptized into Christ have clothed yourselves with Christ" (Galatians 3:27).

"And over all these virtues put on love, which binds them all together in perfect unity" (Colossians 3:14).

LOVE
IS
THE
FRUIT
OF
THE
SPIRIT

But the fruit of the Spirit is love, joy, peace,
forbearance, kindness, goodness, faithfulness.

—Galatians 5:22

Love Is the Fruit of the Spirit

"But the fruit of the Spirit is love, joy, peace, forbearance, kindness, goodness, faithfulness" (Galatians 5:22).

"By their fruit you will recognize them. Do people pick grapes from thorn bushes, or figs from thistles?" (Matthew 7:16).

"Likewise, every good tree bears good fruit, but a bad tree bears bad fruit" (Matthew 7:17).

"A good tree cannot bear bad fruit, and a bad tree cannot bear good fruit" (Matthew 7:18).

"Every tree that does not bear good fruit is cut down and thrown into the fire" (Matthew 7:19).

"For the fruit of the light consists in all goodness, righteousness and truth" (Ephesians 5:9).

"Have nothing to do with fruitless deeds of darkness, but rather expose them" (Ephesians 5:11).

"So I say, walk by the Spirit, and you will not gratify the desires of the flesh" (Galatians 5:16).

"For the flesh desires what is contrary to the Spirit, and the Spirit what is contrary to the flesh. They are conflict with each other so that you are not to do whatever you want" (Galatians 5:17).

"Let us not become conceited, provoking and envying each other" (Galatians 5:26).

"Do nothing out of selfish ambition or vain conceit. Rather, in humility value others above yourselves" (Philippians 2:3).

"Let us not become weary in doing good, for at the proper time we will reap a harvest if we do not give up" (Galatians 6:9).

"Therefore, as we have opportunity, let us do good to all people, especially to those who belong to the family of believers" (Galatians 6:10).

"Since we live by the Spirit, let us keep in step with the Spirit" (Galatians 5:25)

"Bear with each other and forgive one another if any of you has a grievance against someone. Forgive as the Lord forgave you" (Colossians 3:13).

"Let the peace of Christ rule in your hearts, since as members of one body you were called to peace. And be thankful" (Colossians 3:15).

"So that you may live a life worthy of the Lord and please him in every way: bearing fruit in every good work, growing in the knowledge of God" (Colossians 1:10).

FAITH
HOPE
AND
LOVE

And now these three remain: faith, hope and
love. But the greatest of these is love.

—1 Corinthians 13:13

Faith, Hope, and Love

"If I speak in the tongues of men or of angels, but do not have love, I am only a resounding gong or a clanging cymbal" (1 Corinthians 13:1).

"If I have the gift of prophecy and can fathom all mysteries and all knowledge, and if I have a faith that can move mountains, but do not have love, I am nothing" (1 Corinthians 13:2).

"For anyone who speaks in a tongue does not speak to people but to God. Indeed, no one understands them, they utter mysteries by the Spirit" (1 Corinthians 14:2).

"If I give all I possess to the poor and give over my body to hardship that I may boast, but do not have love, I gain nothing" (1 Corinthians 13:3).

"Love is patient, love is kind. It does not envy, it does not boast, it is not proud" (1 Corinthians 13:4).

"And we urge you, brothers and sisters, warn those who are idle and disruptive, encourage the disheartened, help the weak, be patient with everyone" (1 Thessalonians 5:14).

"Love, it does not dishonor others, it is not self-seeking, it is not easily angered, it keeps no record of wrongs" (1 Corinthians 13:5).

"No one should seek their own good, but the good of others" (1 Corinthians 10:24).

"Love does not delight in evil but rejoices with the truth" (1 Corinthians 13:6).

"Love always protects, always trusts, always hopes, always perseveres" (1 Corinthians 13:7).

"Love never fails. But where there are prophecies, they will cease; where there are tongues, they will be stilled; where there is knowledge, it will pass away" (1 Corinthians 13:8).

"Those who think they know something do not yet know as they ought to know" (1 Corinthians 8:2).

"For we live by faith, not by sight" (2 Corinthians 5:7).

"For through the Spirit we eagerly await by faith the righteousness for which we hope" (Galatians 5:5).

"For in this hope we were saved. But hope that is seen is no hope at all. Who hopes for what they already have?" (Romans 8:24).

"But if we hope for what we do not yet have, we wait for it patiently" (Romans 8:25).

"But since we belong to the day, let us be sober, putting on faith and love as a breastplate, and the hope of salvation as a helmet" (1 Thessalonians 5:8).

"For in Christ Jesus neither circumcision nor uncircumcision has any value. The only thing that counts is faith expressing itself through love" (Galatians 5:6).

"And now these three remain: faith, hope and love. But the greatest of these is love" (1 Corinthians 13:13).

"Do everything in love" (1 Corinthians 16:14).

THE
FATHER
ONE
LORD
ONE
FAITH
ONE
BAPTISM

One God and Father of all, who is over
all and through all and in all.

—Ephesians 4:6

The Father One Lord, One Faith, One Baptism

"Therefore, as God's chosen people, holy and dearly loved, clothe yourselves with compassion, kindness, humility, gentleness and patience" (Colossians 3:12).

"Be completely humble and gentle; be patient, bearing with one another in love" (Ephesians 4:2).

"Bear with each other and forgive one another if any of you has a grievance against someone. Forgive as the Lord forgave you" (Colossians 3:13).

"For he chose us in him before the creation of the world to be holy and blameless in his sight. In love" (Ephesians 1:4).

"Make every effort to keep the unity of the Spirit through the bond of peace" (Ephesians 4:3).

"And over all these virtues put on love, which binds them all together in perfect unity" (Colossians 3:14).

"There is one body and one Spirit, just as you were called to one hope when you were called" (Ephesians 4:4).

"One God and Father of all, who is over all and through all and in all" (Ephesians 4:6).

"But to each one of us grace has been given as Christ apportioned it" (Ephesians 4:7).

"Now to each one the manifestation of the Spirit is given for the common good" (1 Corinthians 12:7).

"All these are the work of one and the same Spirit, and he distributes them to each one, just as he determines" (1 Corinthians 12:11).

"For by the grace given me I say to every one of you: Do not think of yourself more highly than you ought, but rather think of yourself with sober judgement, in accordance with the faith God has distributed to each of you" (Romans 12:3).

"Now you are the body of Christ, and each one of you is a part of it" (1 Corinthians 12:27).

"Until we all reach unity in the faith and in the knowledge of the Son of God and become mature, attaining to the whole measure of the fullness of Christ" (Ephesians 4:13).

"For in the gospel the righteousness of God is revealed a righteousness that is by faith from first to last, just as it is written: The righteous will live by faith" (Romans 1:17).

"Therefore, since we have been justified through faith, we have peace with God through our Lord Jesus Christ" (Romans 5:1).

AMBASSADORS
OF
THE
FATHER'S
LOVE

We are therefore Christ's ambassadors, as though
God were making his appeal through us. We implore
you on Christ's behalf: Be reconciled to God.

—2 Corinthians 5:20

Ambassadors of the Father's Love

"For Christ's love compels us, because we are convinced that one died for all, and therefore all died" (2 Corinthians 5:14).

"I have been crucified with Christ and I no longer live, but Christ lives in me. The life I now live in the body, I live by faith in the Son of God, who loved me and gave himself for me" (Galatians 2:20).

"And he died for all, that those who live should no longer live for themselves but for him who died for them and was raised again" (2 Corinthians 5:15).

"For none of us lives for ourselves alone, and none of us dies for ourselves alone" (Romans 14:7).

"If we live, we live for the Lord; and if we die, we die for the Lord. So, whether we live or die, we belong to the Lord" (Romans 14:8).

"For this very reason, Christ died and returned to life so that he might be the Lord of both the dead and the living" (Romans 14:9).

"Therefore, if anyone is in Christ, the new creation has come: The old has gone, the new is here!" (2 Corinthians 5:17).

"Neither circumcision nor uncircumcision means anything; what counts is the new creation" (Galatians 6:15).

"All this is from God, who reconciled us to himself through Christ and gave us the ministry of reconciliation" (2 Corinthians 5:18).

"For if, while we were God's enemies, we were reconciled to him through the death of his Son, how much more, having been reconciled, shall we be saved through his life" (Romans 5:10).

"Not only is this so, but we also boast in God through our Lord Jesus Christ, through whom we have now received reconciliation" (Romans 5:11).

"And through him to reconcile to himself all things, whether things on earth or things in heaven, by making peace through his blood, shed on the cross" (Colossians 1:20).

"But God demonstrates his own love for us in this: While we were still sinners, Christ died for us" (Romans 5:8).

"That God was reconciling the world to himself in Christ, not counting people's sins against them. And he has committed to us the message of reconciliation" (2 Corinthians 5:19).

"Blessed is the one whose sin the Lord will never count against them" (Romans 4:8).

"As God's co-workers we urge you not to receive God's grace in vain" (2 Corinthians 6:1).

"God made him who had no sin to be sin for us, so that in him we might become the righteousness of God" (2 Corinthians 5:21).

"For we do not have a high priest who is unable to empathize with our weaknesses, but we have one who has been tempted in every way, just as we are yet he did not sin" (Hebrews 4:15).

"He committed no sin, and no deceit was found in his mouth" (1 Peter 2:22).

"He himself bore our sins in his body on the cross, so that we might die to sins and live for righteousness, by his wounds you have been healed" (1 Peter 2:24).

"We are therefore Christ's ambassadors, as though God were making his appeal through us. We implore you on Christ's behalf: Be reconciled to God" (2 Corinthians 5:20).

THE
SPIRIT
OF
LOVE
DOES
NOT
CONDEMNS

Therefore, there is now no condemnation
for those who are in Christ Jesus.

—Romans 8:1

The Spirit of Love Does Not Condemns

"Therefore, there is now no condemnation for those who are in Christ Jesus" (Romans 8:1).

"Who then is the one who condemns? No one. Christ Jesus who died more than that, who was raised to life is at the right hand of God and is also interceding for us" (Romans 8:34).

"Whoever believes in him is not condemned, but whoever does not believe stands condemned already because they have not believed in the name of God's one and only Son" (John 3:18).

"Neither height nor depth, nor anything else in all creation, will be able to separate us from the love of God that is in Christ Jesus our Lord" (Romans 8:39).

"Because through Christ Jesus the law of the Spirit who gives life has set you free from the law of sin and death" (Romans 8:2).

"You have been set free from sin and have become slaves to righteousness" (Romans 6:18).

"So, my brothers and sisters, you also died to the law through the body of Christ, that you might belong to another, to him who was raised from the dead, in order that we might bear fruit for God" (Romans 7:4).

"For what the law was powerless to do because it was weakened by the flesh, God did by sending his own Son in the likeness of sinful flesh to be a sin offering and so he condemned sin in the flesh" (Romans 8:3).

"Through him everyone who believes is set free from every sin, a justification you were not able to obtain under the law of Moses" (Acts 13:39).

"Rather, he made himself nothing by taking the very nature of a servant, being made in human likeness" (Philippians 2:7).

"Since the children have flesh and blood, he too shared in their humanity so that by his death he might break the power of him who holds the power of death that is, the devil" (Hebrews 2:14).

"For this reason he had to be made like them, fully human in every way, in order that he might become a merciful and faithful high priest in service to God, and that he might make atonement for the sins of the people" (Hebrews 2:17).

"In order that the righteous requirement of the law might be fully met in us, who do not live according to the flesh but according to the Spirit" (Romans 8:4).

"So I say, walk by the Spirit, and you will not gratify the desires of the flesh" (Galatians 5:16).

"Those who live according to the flesh have their minds set on what the flesh desires; but those who live in accordance with the Spirit have their minds set on what the Spirit desires" (Romans 8:5).

"Those who belong to Christ Jesus have crucified the flesh with its passions and desires" (Galatians 5:24).

"The mind governed by the flesh is death, but the mind governed by the Spirit is life and peace" (Romans 8:6).

"Whoever sows to please their flesh, from the flesh will reap destruction; whoever sows to please the Spirit, from the Spirit will reap eternal life" (Galatians 6:8).

"The mind governed by the flesh is hostile to God; it does not submit to God's law, nor can it do so" (Romans 8:7).

"Those who are in the realm of the flesh cannot please God" (Romans 8:8).

"You, however, are not in the realm of the flesh but are in the realm of the Spirit, if indeed the Spirit of God lives in you. And if anyone does not have the Spirit of Christ, they do not belong to Christ" (Romans 8:9).

"Do you not know that your bodies are temples of the Holy Spirit, who is in you, whom you have received from God? You are not your own" (1 Corinthians 6:19).

"The Spirit of truth. The world cannot accept him because it neither sees him nor knows him. But you know him, for he lives with you and will be in you" (John 14:17).

"This is how we know that we live in him and he in us: He has given us of his Spirit" (1 John 4:13).

"But if Christ is in you, then even though your body is subject to death because of sin, the Spirit gives life because of righteousness" (Romans 8:10).

"And if the Spirit of him who raised Jesus from the dead is living in you, he who raised Christ from the dead will also give life to your mortal bodies because of his Spirit who lives in you" (Romans 8:11).

"But God raised him from the dead, freeing him from the agony of death, because it was impossible for death to keep its hold on him" (Acts 2:24).

"Therefore, brothers and sisters, we have an obligation; but it is not to the flesh, to live according to it" (Romans 8:12).

"For if you live according to the flesh, you will die; but if by the Spirit you put to death the misdeeds of the body, you will live" (Romans 8:13).

"For those who are led by the Spirit of God are the children of God" (Romans 8:14).

"But if you are led by the Spirit, you are not under the law" (Galatians 5:18).

"Yet to all who did receive him, to those who believed in his name, he gave the right to become children of God" (John 1:12).

"The Spirit you received does not make you slaves, so that you live in fear again, rather the Spirit you received brought about your adoption to sonship. And by him we cry "Abba, Father'" (Romans 8:15).

"For the Spirit God gave us does not make us timid, but gives us power, love and self-discipline" (2 Timothy 1:7).

"Because you are his sons, God sent the Spirit of his Son into our hearts, the Spirit who calls out. "Abba Father'" (Galatians 4:6).

"The Spirit himself testifies with our spirit that we are God's children" (Romans 8:16).

"And you also were included in Christ when you heard the message of truth, the gospel of your salvation. When you believed, you were marked in him with a seal, the promised Holy Spirit" (Ephesians 1:13).

"Now if we are children, then we are heirs, heirs of God and co-heirs with Christ, if indeed we share in his sufferings in order that we may also share in his glory" (Romans 8:17).

"For our light and momentary troubles are achieving for us an eternal glory that far outweighs them all" (2 Corinthians 4:17).

"Now the one who has fashioned us for this very purpose is God, who has given us the Spirit as a deposit, guaranteeing what is to come" (2 Corinthians 5:5).

"In the same way, the Spirit helps us in our weakness. We do not know what we ought to pray for, but the Spirit himself intercedes for us through wordless groans" (Romans 8:26).

"And he who searches our hearts knows the mind of the Spirit, because the Spirit intercedes for God's people in accordance with the will of God" (Romans 8:27).

"And pray in the Spirit on all occasions with all kinds of prayers and requests. With this in mind be alert and always keep on praying for all the Lord's people" (Ephesians 6:18).

"For through him we both have access to the Father by one Spirit" (Ephesians 2:18).

POWER
OF
THE
FATHER'S
LOVE

For the kingdom of God is not a matter of talk but of power.

—1 Corinthians 4:20

Power of the Father's Love

"And we know that in all things God works for the good of those who love him, who have been called according to his purpose" (Romans 8:28).

"God is faithful, who has called you into fellowship with his Son, Jesus Christ our Lord" (1 Corinthians 1:9).

"He has saved us and called us to a holy life not because of anything we have done but because of his own purpose and grace. This grace was given us in Christ Jesus before the beginning of time" (2 Timothy 1:9).

"For those God fore-knew he also predestined to be conformed to the image of his Son. That he might be the firstborn among many brothers and sisters" (Romans 8:29).

"In him we were also chosen, having been predestined according to the plan of him who works out everything in conformity with the purpose of his will" (Ephesians 1:11).

"And just as we have borne the image of the earthly man, so shall we bear the image of the heavenly man" (1 Corinthians 15:49).

"And we all, who with unveiled faces contemplate the Lord's glory, are being transformed into his image with ever-increasing glory, which comes from the Lord, who is the Spirit" (2 Corinthians 3:18).

"Who, by the power that enables him to bring everything under his control, will transform our lowly bodies so that they will be like his glorious body" (Philippians 3:21).

"Dear friends, now we are children of God and what we will be, has not yet been made know. But we know that when Christ appears. We shall be like him, for we shall see him as he is" (1 John 3:2).

"And those he predestined, he also called; those he called; he also justified; those he justified, he also glorified" (Romans 8:30).

"He predestined us for adoption to sonship through Jesus Christ, in accordance with his pleasure and will" (Ephesians 1:5).

"And that is what some of you were. But you were washed, you were sanctified, you were justified in the named, of the Lord Jesus Christ and by the Spirit of our God" (1 Corinthians 6:11).

"What, then, shall we say in response to these things? If God is for us, who can be against us?" (Romans 8:31).

"He who did not spare his own Son, but gave him up for us all how will he not also, along with him, graciously give us all things?" (Romans 8:32).

"For God so loved the world that he gave his one and only Son, that whoever believes in him shall not perish but have eternal life" (John 3:16).

"He was delivered over to death for our sins and was raised to life for our justification" (Romans 4:25).

"Who will bring any charge against those whom God has chosen? It is God who justifies" (Romans 8:33).

"Who then is the one who condemns? No one. Christ Jesus who died more than that, who was raised to life is at the right hand of God and is also interceding for us" (Romans 8:34).

"But God demonstrates his own love for us in this: while we were still sinners, Christ died for us" (Romans 5:8).

"My dear children, I write this to you so that you will not sin. But if anybody does sin, we have an advocate with the Father Jesus Christ, the Righteous One" (1 John 2:1)

"I have been crucified with Christ and I no longer live, but Christ lives in me. The life I now live in the body, I live by faith in the Son of God, who loved me and gave himself for me" (Galatians 2:20).

"Who shall separate us from the love of Christ? Shall trouble or hardship or persecution or famine or nakedness or danger or sword?" (Romans 8:35)

"No, in all these things we are more than conquerors through him who loved us" (Romans 8:37).

"For I am convinced that neither death nor life, neither angels nor demons, neither the present nor the future, nor any powers" (Romans 8:38).

"Neither height nor depth, nor anything else in all creation, will be able to separate us from the love of God that is in Christ Jesus our Lord" (Romans 8:39).

"But thanks be to God! He gives us the victory through our Lord Jesus Christ" (1 Corinthians 15:57).

CHRIST'S
LOVE
IS
THE
MODEL
FOR
HUMILITY

Take my yoke upon you and learn from me, for I am gentle
and humble in heart, and you will find rest for your souls.

—Matthew 11:29

Christ's Love Is the Model for Humility

"Therefore if you have any encouragement from being united with Christ, if any comfort from his love, if any common sharing in the Spirit, if any tenderness and compassion" (Philippians 2:1).

"Therefore, as God's chosen people, holy and dearly loved, clothe yourselves with compassion, kindness, humility, gentleness and patience" (Colossians 3:12).

"Then make my joy complete by being like-minded, having the same love, being one in spirit and of one mind" (Philippians 2:2).

"Live in harmony with one another. Do not be proud but be willing to associate with people of low position. Do not be conceited" (Romans 12:16).

"Do nothing out of selfish ambition or vain conceit. Rather, in humility value others above yourselves" (Philippians 2:3).

"Let us not become conceited, provoking and envying each other" (Galatians 5:26).

"Be devoted to one another in love. Honor one another above yourselves" (Romans 12:10).

"In the same way, you who are younger, submit yourselves to your elders. All of you, clothe yourselves with humility toward one another, because God opposes the proud but shows favor to the humble" (1 Peter 5:5).

"Take my yoke upon you and learn from me, for I am gentle and humble in heart, and you will find rest for your souls" (Matthew 11:29).

"Who, being in very nature God, did not consider equality with God something to be used to his own advantage" (Philippians 2:6).

"In the beginning was the word, and the word was with God and the word was God" (John 1:1)

"The Word became flesh and made his dwelling among us. We have seen his glory, the glory of the one and only Son, who came from the Father, full of grace and truth" (John 1:14).

"Rather, he made himself nothing by taking the very nature of a servant, being made in human likeness" (Philippians 2:7).

"For this reason he had to be made like them, fully human in every way, in order that he might become a merciful and faithful high priest in service to God, and that he might make atonement for the sins of the people" (Hebrews 2:17).

"Just as the Son of Man did not come to be served, but to serve, and to give his life as a ransom for many" (Matthew 20:28).

"And being found in appearance as a man, he humbled himself by becoming obedient to death even death on a cross!" (Philippians 2:8).

"Therefore God exalted him to the highest place and gave him the name that is above every name" (Philippians 2:9).

"Far above all rule and authority, power and dominion, and every name that is invoked, not only in the present age but also in the one to come" (Ephesians 1:21).

"Exalted to the right hand of God, he has received from the Father the promised Holy Spirit and has poured out what you now see and hear" (Acts 2:33).

"That at the name of Jesus every knee should bow, in heaven and on earth and under the earth" (Philippians 2:10).

"And every tongue acknowledge that Jesus Christ is Lord, to the glory of God the Father" (Philippians 2:11).

"May the grace of the Lord Jesus Christ, and the love of God, and the fellowship of the Holy Spirit, be with you all" (2 Corinthians 13:14).

"In your relationships with one another, have the same mindset as Christ Jesus" (Philippians 2:5).

Put
on
the
Armor
of
Love

Put on the full armor of God so that you can take
your stand against the devil's schemes.

—Ephesians 6:11

Put on the Armor of Love

"Finally, be strong in the Lord and in his mighty power" (Ephesians 6:10).

"Be on your guard; stand firm in the faith; be courageous; be strong" (1 Corinthians 16:13).

"And his incomparably great power for us who believe. That power is the same as the mighty strength" (Ephesians 1:19).

"Put on the full armor of God, so that you can take your stand against the devil's schemes" (Ephesians 6:11).

"The night is nearly over; the day is almost here so let us put aside the deeds of darkness and put on the armor of light" (Romans 13:12).

"For our struggle is not against flesh and blood, but against the rulers, against the authorities, against the powers of this dark world and against the spiritual forces of evil in the heavenly realms" (Ephesians 6:12).

"For I am convinced that neither death nor life, neither angels nor demons, neither the present nor the future, nor any powers" (Romans 8:38).

"Neither height nor depth, nor anything else in all creation, will be able to separate us from the love of God that is in Christ Jesus our Lord" (Romans 8:39).

"Praise be to the God and Father of our Lord Jesus Christ, who has blessed us in the heavenly realms with every spiritual blessing in Christ" (Ephesians 1:3).

"Therefore put on the full armor of God, so that when the day of evil comes, you may be able to stand your ground, and after you have done everything, to stand" (Ephesians 6:13).

"Stand firm then, with the belt of truth buckled around your waist, with the breastplate of righteousness in place" (Ephesians 6:14).

"And with your feet fitted with the readiness that comes from the gospel of peace" (Ephesians 6:15).

"How beautiful on the mountains are the feet of those who bring good news, who proclaim peace, who bring good tidings, who proclaim salvation, who say to Zion, Your God reigns!" (Isaiah 52:7).

"In addition to all this, take up the shield of faith, with which you can extinguish all the flaming arrows of the evil one" (Ephesians 6:16).

"Take the helmet of salvation and the sword of the Spirit, which is the word of God" (Ephesians 6:17).

"For the word of God is alive and active. Sharper than any double-edged sword, it penetrates even to dividing soul and spirit, joints and marrow; it judges the thoughts and attitudes of the heart" (Hebrews 4:12).

"Watch and pray so that you will not fall into temptation. The spirit is willing, but the flesh is weak" (Matthew 26:41).

"And pray in the Spirit on all occasions with all kinds of prayers and requests. with this in mind be alert and always keep on praying for all the Lord's people" (Ephesians 6:18).

"May God himself, the God of peace, sanctify you through and through. May your whole spirit, soul and body be kept blameless at the coming of our Lord Jesus Christ" (1 Thessalonians 5:23).

"For everyone born of God overcomes the world. This is the victory that has overcome the world, even our faith" (1 John 5:4).

THE
FATHER
OF
LOVE
DISCIPLINES

Because the Lord disciplines one he loves, and he
chastens everyone he accepts as his son.

—Hebrews 12:6

The Father of Love Disciplines

"Therefore, since we are surrounded by such a great cloud of witnesses, let us throw off everything that hinders and the sin that so easily entangles. And let us run with perseverance the race marked out for us" (Hebrews 12:1).

"Do you not know that in a race all the runners run, but only one gets the prize? Run in such a way as to get the prize" (1 Corinthians 9:24).

"You need to persevere so that when you have done the will of God, you will receive what he has promised" (Hebrews 10:36).

"Fixing our eyes on Jesus, the pioneer and perfecter of faith. For the joy set before him he endured the cross, scorning its shame, and set down at the right hand of the throne of God" (Hebrews 12:2).

"And being found in appearance as a man, he humbled himself by becoming obedient to death even death on a cross!" (Philippians 2:8).

"Therefore God exalted him to the highest place and gave him the name that is above every name" (Philippians 2:9).

"Consider him who endured such opposition from sinners, so that you will not grow weary and lose heart" (Hebrews 12:3).

"Let us not become weary in doing good, for at the proper time we will reap a harvest if we do not give up" (Galatians 6:9).

"In your struggle against sin, you have not yet resisted to the point of shedding your blood" (Hebrews 12:4).

"Sometimes you were publicly exposed to insult and persecution; at other times you stood side by side with those who were so treated" (Hebrews 10:33).

"Because the Lord disciplines one he loves, and he chastens everyone he accepts as his son" (Hebrews 12:6).

"Moreover, we have all had human fathers who disciplined us, and we respected them for it. How much more should we submit to the Father of spirits and live" (Hebrews 12:9).

"They disciplined us for a little while as they thought best; but God disciplines us for our good, in order that we may share in his holiness" (Hebrews 12:10).

"Through these he has given us his very great and precious promises, so that through them you may participate in the divine nature, having escaped the corruption in the world caused by evil desires" (2 Peter 1:4).

"Resist him, standing firm in the faith, because you know that the family of believers throughout the world is undergoing the same kind of sufferings" (1 Peter 5:9).

"No discipline seems pleasant at the time, but painful. Later however, it produces a harvest of righteousness and peace for those who have been trained by it" (Hebrews 12:11).

"The fruit of that righteousness will be peace; its effect will be quietness and confidence forever" (Isaiah 32:17).

"But the wisdom that comes from heaven is first, of all pure then peace-loving, considerate, submissive, full of mercy and good fruit, impartial and sincere" (James 3:17).

"Peacemakers who sow in peace reap a harvest of righteousness" (James 3:18).

"Give careful thought to the paths for your feet and be steadfast in all your ways" (Proverbs 4:26).

"Make every effect to live in peace with everyone and to be holy; without holiness no one will see the Lord" (Hebrews 12:14).

"But now that you have been set free from sin and have become slaves of God, the benefit you reap leads to holiness, and the result is eternal life" (Romans 6:22).

"Blessed are the peacemakers, for they will be called children of God" (Matthew 5:9).

THE
WORLD'S
WISDOM
IS
FOOLISHNESS
IN
LOVE
SIGHT

For the wisdom of this world is foolishness in God's sight.

—1 Corinthians 3:19

The World's Wisdom Is Foolishness in Love Sight

"Do not deceive yourselves. If any of you think you are wise by the standards of this age, you should become fools so that you may become wise" (1 Corinthians 3:18).

"Woe to those who are wise in their own eyes and clever in their own sight" (Isaiah 5:21).

"Those who think they know something do not yet know as they ought to know" (1 Corinthians 8:2).

"For the wisdom of this world is foolishness in God's sight. As it is written: He catches the wise in their craftiness" (1 Corinthians 3:19).

"But God chose the foolish things of the world to shame the wise; God chose the weak things of the world to shame the strong" (1 Corinthians 1:27).

"The LORD knows all human plans; he knows that they are futile" (Psalm 94:11).

"The fear of the LORD is the beginning of knowledge, but fools despise wisdom and instruction" (Proverbs 1:7).

"For the message of the cross is foolishness to those who are perishing, but to us who are being saved it is the power of God" (1 Corinthians 1:18).

"For I am not ashamed of the gospel, because it is the power of God that brings salvation to everyone who believes: first to the Jew, then to the Gentile" (Romans 1:16).

"For we are to God the pleasing aroma of Christ among those who are being saved and those who are perishing" (2 Corinthians 2:15).

"What we have received is not the spirit of the world, but the Spirit who is from God, so that we may understand what God has freely given us" (1 Corinthians 2:12).

"This is what we speak, not in words taught us by human wisdom but in words taught by the Spirit, explaining spiritual realities with Spirit-taught words" (1 Corinthians 2:13).

"The person without the Spirit does not accept the things that come from the Spirit of God but considers them foolishness and cannot understand them because they are discerned only through the Spirit" (1 Corinthians 2:14).

"But to those whom God has called, both Jews and Greeks, Christ the power of God and the wisdom of God" (1 Corinthians 1:24).

"Trust in the LORD with all your heart and lean not to your own understanding" (Proverbs 3:5).

"In all your ways submit to him, and he will make your paths straight" (Proverbs 3:6).

"Do not be wise in your own eyes; fear the LORD and shun evil" (Proverbs 3:7).

"This will bring health to your body and nourishment to your bones" (Proverbs 3:8).

"By wisdom the LORD laid the earth's foundations, by understanding he set the heavens in place" (Proverbs 3:19).

THE
FATHER
OF
LOVE
WISDOM
VERSUS
EARTHLY
WISDOM

But the wisdom that comes from heaven is first pure,
then peace-loving, considerate, submissive, full of
mercy and good fruit, impartial and sincere.

—James 3:17

The Father of Love Wisdom versus Earthly Wisdom

"Who is wise and understanding among you? Let them show it by their good life, by deeds done in the humility that comes from wisdom" (James 3:13).

"But someone will say, you have faith; I have deeds. Show me your faith without deeds, and I will show you my faith by my deeds" (James 2:18).

"But if you harbor bitter envy selfish ambition in your hearts, do not boast about it or deny the truth" (James 3:14).

"For where you have envy and selfish ambition, there you find disorder and every evil practice" (James 3:16).

"Such wisdom does not come down from heaven but is earthly, unspiritual, demonic" (James 3:15).

"The Spirit clearly says that in later times some will abandon the faith and follow deceiving spirits and things taught by demons" (1 Timothy 4:1).

"We do, however, speak a message of wisdom among the mature, but not the wisdom of this age or of the rulers of this age, who are coming to nothing" (1 Corinthians 2:6).

"Every good and perfect gift is from above, coming down from the Father of the heavenly lights, who does not change like shifting shadows" (James 1:17).

"Love must be sincere. Hate what is evil; cling to what is good" (Romans 12:9).

"But the wisdom that comes from heaven is first pure, then peace-loving, considerate, submissive, full of mercy and good fruit, impartial and sincere" (James 3:17).

"Peacemakers who sow in peace reap a harvest of righteousness" (James 3:18).

"Blessed are those who find wisdom, those who gain understanding" (Proverbs 3:13).

"For she is more profitable than silver and yields better returns than gold" (Proverbs 3:14).

"She is more precious than rubies; nothing you desire can compare with her" (Proverbs 3:15).

"Long life is in her right hand; in her left hand are riches and honor" (Proverbs 3:16).

"Her ways are pleasant ways, and all her paths are peace" (Proverbs 3:17).

"She is a tree of life to those who take hold of her; those who hold her fast will be blessed" (Proverbs 3:18).

THE
FATHER'S
LOVE
IN
MARRIAGE

In the same way, husband's ought to love their wives as
their own bodies. He who loves his wife love himself.

—Ephesians 5:28

The Father's Love in Marriage

"Wives in the same way submit yourselves to your own husbands so that, if any of them do not believe the word, they may be won over without words by the behavior of their wives" (1 Peter 3:1).

"Wives submit yourselves to your own husbands as you do to the Lord" (Ephesians 5:22).

"How do you know, wife, whether you will save your husband? Or, how do you know, husband, whether you will save your wife?" (1 Corinthians 7:16).

"When they see the purity and reverence of your lives" (1 Peter 3:2).

"Your beauty should not come from outward adornment, such as elaborate hairstyles and the wearing of gold jewelry or fine clothes" (1 Peter 3:3).

"Rather it should be that of your inner self, the unfading beauty of a gentle and quiet spirit, which is of great worth in God's sight" (1 Peter 3:4).

"For this the way holy women of the past who put their hope in God used to adorn themselves. They submitted themselves to their own husbands" (1 Peter 3:5).

"Husbands, in the same way be considerate as you live with your wives; and treat them with respect as the weaker partner and as heirs with you of the gracious gift of life, so that nothing will hinder your prayers" (1 Peter 3:7).

"Husbands, love your wives and do not be harsh with them" (Colossians 3:19).

"Husbands, love your wives, just as Christ loved the church and gave himself up for her" (Ephesians 5:25).

"To make her holy, cleansing her by the washing with water through the word" (Ephesians 5:26).

"And to present her to himself as a radiant church, without stain or wrinkle or any other blemish, but holy and blameless" (Ephesians 5:27).

"And walk in the way of love, just as Christ loved us and gave himself up for us as a fragrant offering and sacrifice to God" (Ephesians 5:2).

"For he chose us in him before the creation of the world to be holy and blameless in his sight. In love" (Ephesians 1:4).

"But now he his reconciled you by Christ's physical body through death to present you holy in his sight, without blemish and free from accusation" (Colossians 1:22).

"In this same way; husbands ought to love their wives as their own bodies. He who loves his wife love himself" (Ephesians 5:28).

"After all, no one ever hated their own body, but they feed and care for their body, just as Christ does the church" (Ephesians 5:29).

"For we are members of his body" (Ephesians 5:30).

"This reason a man will leave his father and mother and be united to his wife, and the two will become one flesh" (Ephesians 5:31).

"However, each one of you also must love his wife as he loves himself, and the wife must respect her husband" (Ephesians 5:33).

"Now you are the body of Christ, and each one of you is a part of it" (1 Corinthians 12:27).

"Be devoted to one another in love. Honor one another above yourselves" (Romans 12:10).

"Love must be sincere. Hate what is evil; cling to what is good" (Romans 12:9).

You
Are
the
Light
of
Love
in
the
World

You are the light of the world. A town
built on hill cannot be hidden.

—Matthew 5:14

You Are the Light of Love in the World

"My dear children, I write this to you so that you will not sin. But if anybody does sin, we have an advocate with the Father Jesus Christ, the Righteous One" (1 John 2:1).

"I am writing to you, dear children, because your sins have been forgiven on account of his name" (1 John 2:12).

"Who then is the one who condemns? No one. Christ Jesus who died more than that, who was raised to life is at the right hand of God and is also interceding for us" (Romans 8:34).

"Therefore he is able, to save completely those who come to God through him, because he always lives to intercede for them" (Hebrews 7:25).

"He is the atoning sacrifice for our sins, and not only for ours but also for the sins of the whole world" (1 John 2:2).

"God presented Christ as a sacrifice of atonement, through the shedding of his blood to be received by faith. He did this to demonstrate his righteousness, because in his forbearance he had left the sins committed beforehand unpunished" (Romans 3:25).

"We know that we have come to know him if we keep his commands" (1 John 2:3).

"If you love me, keep my commands" (John 14:15).

"Whoever says, I know him but does not do what He commands is a liar; and the truth is not in that person" (1 John 2:4).

"If we claim to have fellowship with him and yet walk in the darkness, we lie and do not live out the truth" (1 John 1:6).

"If we claim to be without sin, we deceive ourselves and the truth is not in us" (1 John 1:8).

"But anyone obeys his word, love for God is truly made complete in them. This is how we know we are in him" (1 John 2:5).

"Whoever has my commands and keeps them is the one who loves me. The one who loves me will be loved by my Father, and I too will love them and show myself to them" (John 14:21).

"Jesus replied, anyone who loves me will obey my teaching. My Father will love them, and we will come to them and make our home with them" (John 14:23).

"No one has ever seen God; but if we love one another, God lives in us and his love is made complete in us" (1 John 4:12).

"Whoever claims to live in him must live as Jesus did" (1 John 2:6).

"Take my yoke upon you and learn from me, for I am gentle and humble in heart, and you will find rest for your souls" (Matthew 11:29).

"To this you were called, because Christ suffered for you, leaving you an example, that you should follow in his steps" (1 Peter 2:21).

"Dear friends, I am not writing you a new command but an old one, which you have had since the beginning" (1 John 2:7).

"And this is his command: to believe in the name of his Son, Jesus Christ, and to love one another as he commanded us" (1 John 3:23).

"Yet I am writing you a new command; its truth is seen in him and in you, because the darkness is passing, and the true light is already shining" (1 John 2:8).

"A new command I give you: Love one another. As I have loved you, so you must love one another" (John 13:34).

"The night is nearly over; the day is almost here, so let us put aside the deeds of darkness and put on the armor of light" (Romans 13:12).

"The true light that gives light to everyone was coming into the world" (John 1:9).

"For you were once darkness, but now you are light in the Lord. Live as children of Light" (Ephesians 5:8).

"You are all children of the light and children of the day. We do not belong to the night or to the darkness" (1 Thessalonians 5:5).

"Anyone who loves their brother and sister lives in the light, and there is nothing in them to make them stumble" (1 John 2:10).

"We know that we have passed from death to life, because we love each other. Anyone who does not love remains in death" (1 John 3:14).

"But anyone who hates a brother or sister is in the darkness and walks around in the darkness. They do not know where they are going, because the darkness has blinded them" (1 John 2:11).

"Then Jesus told them, "You are going to have the light just a little while longer. Walk while you have the light, before darkness overtakes you. Whoever walks in the dark does not know where they are going" (John 12:35).

"Believe in the light while you have the light, so that you may become children of light" (John 12:36).

JESUS
THE
TRUE
LIGHT
THAT
GIVES
LIFE
TO
THE
WORLD

Jesus said I am the light of the world. Whoever follows me will never, walk in darkness but will have the light of life.

—John 8:12

Jesus the True Light That Gives Life to the World

"Jesus answered, I am the way and the truth and the life. No one comes to the Father except through me" (John 14:6).

"Jesus said I am the light of the world. Whoever follows me will never, walk in darkness but will have the light of life" (John 8:12).

"In him was life and that life was the light of all mankind" (John 1:4).

"The light shines in the darkness, and the darkness has not overcome it" (John 1:5).

"He was in the world, and though the world was made through him, the world did not recognize him" (John 1:10).

"He came to that which was his own, but his own did not receive him" (John 1:11).

"This is the verdict: Light has come into the world, but people loved darkness instead of light because their deeds were evil" (John 3:19).

"Everyone who does evil hates the light and will not come into the light for fear that their deeds will be exposed" (John 3:20).

"But whoever lives by the truth comes into the light, so that it may be seen plainly that what they have done has been done in the sight of God" (John 3:21).

"For God, who said, let light shine out of darkness made his light shine in our hearts to give us the light of the knowledge of God's glory displayed in the face of Christ" (2 Corinthians 4:6).

"The LORD is my light and my salvation whom shall; I fear? The LORD is the stronghold of my life of whom shall I be afraid?" (Psalm 27:1)

"For you have delivered me from death and my feet from stumbling, that I may walk before God in the light of life" (Psalm 56:13).

"The city does not need the sun or the moon to shine on it, for the glory of God gives it light, and the Lamb (Jesus) is its lamp" (Revelation 21:23).

"The sun will no more be your light by day, nor will the brightness of the moon shine on you, for the LORD will be your everlasting light, and your God will be your glory" (Isaiah 60:19).

"Arise, shine, for your light has come, and the glory of the LORD rises upon you" (Isaiah 60:1).

"For the LORD God is a sun and shield, the LORD bestows favor and honor; no good thing does he withhold from those whose walk is blameless" (Psalm 84:11).

"Your word is a lamp for my feet, a light on my path" (Psalm 119:105).

"The unfolding of your words gives light; it gives understanding to the simple" (Psalm 119:130).

"God is light in him there is no darkness at all" (1 John 1:5).

"For my yoke is easy and my burden is light" (Matthew 11:30).

"The path of the righteous is like the morning sun, shining ever brighter till the full light of day" (Proverbs 4:18).

DON'T
WORRY
THE
FATHER
WILL
PROVIDE
FOR
YOU

Look at the birds of the air, they do not sow or reap or store away in barns, and yet your heavenly Father feeds them. Are you not much more valuable than they?

—Matthew 6:26

Don't Worry, the Father Will Provide for You

"Therefore I tell you, do not worry about your life, what you will eat or drink; or about your body, what you will wear. Is not life more than food, and the body more than clothes?"[140]

"Can any one of you by worrying add a single hour to your life?"[141]

"And why do you worry about clothes? See how the flowers of the field grow. They do not labor or spin."[142]

"So do not worry, saying, what shall we eat? Or what shall we drink? Or what shall we wear?"[143]

"Therefore do not worry about tomorrow, for tomorrow will worry about itself. Each day have enough trouble of its own."[144]

"Martha, Martha, the Lord answered, you are worried and upset about many things."[145]

"Anxiety weighs down the heart, but a kind word cheers it up."[146]

"Do not be anxious about anything, but in every situation, by prayer and petition, with thanksgiving, present your requests to God."[147]

---

[140] Matthew 6:25
[141] Matthew 6:27
[142] Matthew 6:28
[143] Matthew 6:31
[144] Matthew 6:34
[145] Luke 10:41
[146] Proverbs 12:25
[147] Philippians 4:6

"Cast all your anxiety on him because he cares for you."[148]

"Look at the birds of the air; they do not sow or reap or store away in barns, and yet your heavenly Father feeds them. Are you not much more valuable than they?"[149]

"Are not two sparrows sold for a penny? Yet not one of them will fall to the ground outside your Father's care."[150]

"And even the very hairs of your head are all numbered."[151]

"So do not be afraid you are worth more than many sparrows."[152]

"Keep your lives free from the love of money and be content with what you have, because God has said, 'Never will I leave you; never will I forsake you'."[153]

"If that is how God clothes the grass of the field, which is here today and tomorrow is thrown into the fire, will he not much more clothe you. You of little faith?"[154]

"But seek first his kingdom and his righteousness, and all these things will be given to you as well."[155]

"Ask and it will be given to you; seek and you find; knock and the door will be opened to you."[156]

"For everyone who asks receives; the one who seeks finds; and the one who knocks the door will be opened."[157] .

"If you believe, you will receive whatever you ask for in prayer."[158]

"The blessing of the LORD brings wealth, without painful toil for it."[159]

---

[148] 1 Peter 5:7
[149] Matthew 6:26
[150] Matthew 10:29
[151] Matthew 10:30
[152] Matthew 10:31
[153] Hebrews 13:5
[154] Matthew 6:30
[155] Matthew 6:33
[156] Matthew 7:7
[157] Matthew 7:8
[158] Matthew 21:22
[159] Proverbs 10:22

THE
FATHER'S
LOVE
WILL
PROTECT
YOU

God is our refuge and strength, an ever-present help in trouble.

—Psalm 46:1

The Father's Love Will Protect You

"Whoever dwells in the shelter of the Most, High will rest in the shadow of the Almighty."[160]

"In the shelter of your presence, you hide them from all human intrigues; you keep them safe in your dwelling from accusing tongues."[161]

"Keep me as the apple of your eye; hide me in the shadow of your wings."[162]

"I will say of the LORD, He is my refuge and my fortress, my God, in whom I trust."[163]

"I cry to you, LORD; I say, you are my refuge, my portion in the land of the living."[164]

"The eyes of the LORD are on the righteous, and his ears are attentive to their cry."[165]

"Surely! he will save you from the fowler's snare and from the deadly pestilence."[166]

"When famine or plague comes to the land, or when an enemy besieges them in any of their cities, whatever disaster or disease may come."[167]

"He will cover you with his feathers, and under his wings you will find refuge; his faithfulness will be your shield and rampart."[168]

---

[160] Psalm 91:1
[161] Psalm 31:20
[162] Psalm 17:8
[163] Psalm 91:2
[164] Psalm 142:5
[165] Psalm 34:15
[166] Psalm 91:3
[167] 1 Kings 8:37
[168] Psalm 91:4

"You will not fear the terror of night, nor the arrow that flies by day, nor the pestilence that stalks in the darkness, nor the plague that destroys at midday."[169]

"A thousand may fall at your side, ten thousand at your right hand, but it will not come near you."[170]

"You will be protected from the lash of the tongue and need not fear when destruction comes."[171]

"You will only observe with your eyes and see the punishment of the wicked."[172]

"Hope in the LORD and keep in his way. He will exalt you to inherit the land; when the wicked are destroyed, you will see it."[173]

"If you say, The LORD is my refuge, and you make the Most High your dwelling, no harm will overtake you, no disaster will come near your tent."[174]

"No harm overtakes the righteous, but the wicked have their fill of trouble."[175]

"For he will command his angels concerning you to guard you in all your ways."[176]

"The angel of the LORD encamps around those who fear him, and he delivers them."[177]

"They will lift you up in their hands, so that you will not strike your foot against a stone."[178]

"You will tread on the lion and the cobra; you will trample the great lion and the serpent."[179]

---

[169] Psalm 91:5–6
[170] Psalm 91:7
[171] Job 5:21
[172] Psalm 91:8
[173] Psalm 37:34
[174] Psalm 91:9–10
[175] Proverbs 12:21
[176] Psalm 91:11
[177] Psalm 34:7
[178] Psalm 91:12
[179] Psalm 91:13

"I have given you authority to trample on snakes and scorpions and to overcome all the power of the enemy; nothing will harm you."[180]

"Because he loves me, says the LORD, I will rescue him; I will protect him, for he acknowledges my name."[181]

"He will call on me, and I will answer him; I will be with him in trouble, I will deliver him and honor him."[182]

"The righteous person may have many troubles, but the LORD delivers him from them all."[183]

"God is our refuge and strength, an ever-present help in trouble."[184]

"With long life I will satisfy him and show him my salvation."[185]

"The righteous will flourish like a palm tree, they will grow like a cedar of Lebanon; planted in the house of the LORD, they will flourish in the courts of our God."[186]

"They will still bear fruit in old age they will stay fresh and green."[187]

"Love always protects."[188]

---

[180] Luke 10:19
[181] Psalm 91:14
[182] Psalm 91:15
[183] Psalm 34:19
[184] Psalm 46:1
[185] Psalm 91:16
[186] Psalm 92:12–13
[187] Psalm 92:14
[188] 1 Corinthians 13:7

LET
LOVE
LEAD
YOU

For the Lamb at the center of the throne will be their
shepherd he will lead them to springs of living water.
And God will wipe away every tear from their eyes.

—Revelation 7:17

Let Love Lead You

"The LORD is my shepherd, I lack nothing."[189]

"He tends his flock like a shepherd. He gathers the lambs in his arms and carries them close to his heart; he gently leads those that have young."[190]

"I am the good shepherd. The good shepherd lays down his life for the sheep."[191]

"For you were like sheep going astray, but now you have returned to the Shepherd and Overseer of your souls."[192]

"And my God will meet all your needs according to the riches of his glory in Christ Jesus."[193]

"He makes me lie down in green pastures he leads me beside quiet waters."[194]

"For the Lamb at the center of the throne will be their shepherd he will lead them to springs of living water. And God will wipe away every tear from their eyes."[195]

"He refreshes my soul. He guides me along the right paths for his name's sake."[196]

---

[189] Psalm 23:1

[190] Isaiah 40:11

[191] John 10:11

[192] 1 Peter 2:25

[193] Philippians 4:19

[194] Psalm 23:2

[195] Revelation 7:17

[196] Psalm 23:3

"The law of the LORD is perfect, refreshing the soul. The statutes of the LORD are trustworthy, making wise the simple."[197]

"Righteousness goes before him and prepares the way for his steps."[198]

"Even though I walk through the darkest valley, I will fear no evil, for you are with me, your rod and your staff, they comfort me."[199]

"I will not fear though tens of thousands assail me on every side."[200]

"The LORD is my light and my salvation whom shall I fear? The LORD is the stronghold of my life of whom shall I be afraid?"[201]

"When you pass through the waters, I will be with you; and when you pass through the rivers, they will not sweep over you. When you walk through the fire, you will not be burned; the flames will not set you ablaze."[202]

"You prepare a table before me in the presence of my enemies. You anoint my head with oil, my cup overflows."[203]

"LORD, you alone are my portion and my cup; you make my lot secure."[204]

"Surely your goodness and love will follow me all the days of my life, and I will dwell in the house of the LORD forever."[205]

---

[197] Psalm 19:7
[198] Psalm 85:13
[199] Psalm 23:4
[200] Psalm 3:6
[201] Psalm 27:1
[202] Isaiah 43:2
[203] Psalm 23:5
[204] Psalm 16:5
[205] Psalm 23:6

RENEWING
YOUR
MIND
ABOUT
THE SPIRIT, SOUL, AND BODY

May God himself, the God of peace, sanctify you through
and through. May your whole spirit, soul and body be
kept blameless at the coming of the Lord Jesus Christ.
The one who calls you is faithful, and he will do it.

—1 Thessalonians 5:23–24

Renewing Your Mind about the Spirit, Soul, and Body

Dear friend, I pray that you may enjoy good health and that all may go well with you, even as your soul is getting along well.

—3 John 2

Most people believe that as human being, they are only made up of body and soul. They believe that the soul and spirit as being the same thing.

We Are Three-Part Beings

Your spirit is your innermost part the core of your being, the center of who you are which cannot be seen or felt.

Your soul—mind, will, emotions, and conscience is what most people call their personality, which cannot be seen but felt.

Your body is your physical part that you and others can see and feel.

Soul and body

Your body and your soul you can feel by speaking and touching. If I put my hand on your hands, you know that I touched you. I can also touch you whether I am physically near you or not. By speaking to your soul, I can make you happy or sad. My words can hurt you without even touching your physical body. Because you are in constant touch with your body and soul, it is easy to know how you are feeling. Your body takes a mental inventory feeding you the information, telling you how it is feeling. It is the same way with your soul: if you are hurting and having any fear or depression in life, you would know because you are always in touch with your soul.

Spirit to spirit

Your spirit can only be accessed through the Spirit of God. Truth can only be discerned through the Spirit realm. The only way you are going to know what your spirit is like, by studying the word of God and believing in it.

> These are the things God has revealed to us by his Spirit. The Spirit searches all things, even the deep things of God. For who knows a person's thoughts except their own spirit within them? In the same way no one knows the thoughts of God except the Spirit of God. What we have received is not the spirit of the world, but the Spirit who is from God, so that we may understand what God has freely given us. This is what we speak, not in words taught us by human wisdom but in words taught by the Spirit, explaining spiritual realities with Spirit-taught words. (1 Corinthians 2:10–13)

> The Spirit of truth, the world cannot accept him, because it neither sees him nor knows him. But you know him, for he lives with you and will be in you. (John 14:17)

Notice the scripture calls the Spirit "him." There is no direct connection between the spirit and flesh. You cannot contact your spirit through your emotions or your physical body. You must understand that spiritual reality cannot be felt or seen in the natural realm. The only way to spiritual truth is through the Word of God. When you become born again, you are now operating from the kingdom of God system, which is from above heavenly and spiritual. Because God is a Spirit, his Word is your spiritual mirror. The Father sees you through his Son Jesus who is also the Word of God. The Son is the image of the invisible God, the firstborn over all creation. For in him all things were created.

> Anyone who listens to the word but does not do what it says is like someone who looks at his face in a mirror and after looking at himself, goes away and immediately forgets what he looks like. But whoever looks intently into the perfect law that gives freedom and continues in it not forgetting what they have heard but doing it they will be blessed in what they do. (James 1:23–25)

When you are looking in a mirror, what you are seeing is a reflection. The Word of God is your mirror letting you know how you should see yourself as a child of God. You must trust the spiritual reality you see because you walk by faith, not by sight, and receive all he has promised you through his Son Jesus Christ who is the living Word. If you do not understand how the spirit, soul, and body works, you will be confused and become frustrated and will not believe in the Word of God.

> Therefore if any man be in Christ, he is a new creature: old things are passed away; behold, all things are become new. And all things are of God, who hath reconciled us to himself by Jesus Christ. (2 Corinthians 5:17–18)

This scripture is talking about a complete transformation that takes place in your born-again spirit, your soul, and body that has not been changed yet. Children of God will experience change in their souls when they start renewing their minds to the Word of God and believing it.

> Do not conform to the pattern of this world but be transformed by renewing of your mind. Then you will be able to test and approve what God's will is his good, pleasing and perfect will. (Romans 12:2)

> For though we walk in the flesh, we do not war after the flesh. The weapons of our warfare are not carnal, but mighty through God to the pulling down of strong holds. Casting down imaginations, and every high thing that exalt itself against the knowledge of God, bringing into captivity every thought to the obedience of Christ. (2 Corinthians 10:3–5)

> For it is within, out a person's heart, that evil thoughts come. (Mark 7:21)

> To put off your old self, which is being corrupted by its deceitful desires and to be made new in the attitude of your minds; and put on the new self, which is created to be like God in true righteousness and holiness. (Ephesians 4:22–24)

> Then you will know the truth, and the truth will set you free. (John 8:32)

The complete transformation of your soul takes place when you go to be with Jesus; that is when you receive your glorified soul and body. I believe this is the reason why some may lose faith and unbelief takes hold, thinking they are not saved. When you start renewing your mind to the promises of God's Word that you have already received through his Son Jesus Christ and believing in them, you begin to speak and act like your Father God and his Son. Your spirit and soul will start connecting, and your body will have to line up.

The word of God is alive and active. Sharper than any double-edged sword, it penetrates even to dividing soul and spirit, joints and marrow; it judges the thoughts and attitudes of the heart. (Hebrews 4:12)

Examine yourselves to see whether you are in faith; test yourselves. (2 Corinthians 13:5)

What good will it be for someone to gain the whole world, yet forfeit their soul? Or what can anyone give in exchange for their soul? (Matthew 16:26)

Do not be deceived God cannot be mocked. A man reaps what he sows whoever sows to please their flesh, from the flesh will reap destruction. Whoever sows to please the Spirit, from the Spirit will reap eternal life. (Galatians 6:7–8)

That which is known about God is evident to them and made plain in their inner consciousness, because God (Himself) has shown it to them. Since the creation of the world His invisible nature and attributes, that is, His eternal power and divinity, have been made intelligible and clearly discernible in and through the things that have been made (His handiworks) so men are without excuse. (Romans 1:19–20)

Jesus said, "Come to me, all you who are weary and burdened, and I will give you rest. Take my yoke upon you and learn from me, for I am gentle and humble in heart, and you will find rest for your souls." (Matthew 11:28–29)

Now do you see why it is important for you to understand how the spirit, soul, and body works and knowing that you have work to do as well, and that is renewing your mind to the Word of God so your soul can prosper?

Scriptures to Reference

"Create in me a pure heart, O God, and renew a steadfast spirit within me" (Psalm 51:10).

"Like new-born babies, crave pure spiritual milk, so that by it you may grow up in your salvation" (1 Peter 2:2).

"For you were like sheep going astray, but now you have returned to the Shepherd and Overseer of your souls" (1 Peter 2:25).

"Jesus said, 'I am the good shepherd. The good shepherd lays down his life for the sheep'" (John 10:11).

"God the LORD says the Creator of the heavens and earth who gives breath to its people, and life to those who walk on it" (Isaiah 42:5).

"Do not be afraid of those who kill the body but cannot kill the soul. Rather, be afraid of the One who can destroy both soul and body in hell" (Matthew 10:28).

"God is faithful, who has called you into fellowship with his Son, Jesus Christ our Lord" (1 Corinthians 1:9).

"Then God said, 'Let us make mankind in our image, in our likeness, So God created mankind in his own image, in the image of God he created them; male and female he created them'" (Genesis 1:26–27).

"Then the LORD God formed a man from the dust of the ground and breathed into his nostrils the breath of life, and the man became a living being" (Genesis 2:7).

"But it is the spirit in a person, the breath of the Almighty, that gives them understanding" (Job 32:8).

"The Spirit of God has made me; the breath of the Almighty gives me life" (Job 33:4).

"The LORD God caused the man to fall into a deep sleep; and while he was sleeping, he took one of the man's ribs and then closed the place with flesh" (Genesis 2:21).

"Then the LORD God made a woman from the rib he had taken out of the man, and he brought her to the man" (Genesis 2:22).

"The man said, this is now bone of my bones and flesh of my flesh; she shall be called woman, for she was taken out of man" (Genesis 2:23).

"When God created mankind, he made them in the likeness of God. He created them male and female and blessed them. And he named them Mankind when they were created" (Genesis 5:1–2).

"Praise the LORD, my soul; all my inmost being, praise his holy name" (Psalm 103:1).

"Praise the LORD, my soul, and forget not all his benefits" (Psalm 103:2).

"For he knows how we are formed he remembers that we are dust" (Psalm 103:14).

"The God who made the world and everything in it is the Lord of heaven and earth and does not live in; temples built by human hands" (Acts 17:24).

"And he is not served by human hands, as if he needed anything. Rather, he himself gives everyone life and breath and everything else" (Acts 17:25).

"Flesh gives birth to flesh, but the Spirit gives birth to spirit" (John 3:6).

"The Spirit gives life the flesh counts for nothing. The words I have spoken to you they are full of Spirit and life" (John 6:63).

"Jesus answered I am the way and the truth and the life no one comes to the Father except through me" (John 14:6).

"Jesus breathed on them and said, 'Receive the Holy Spirit'" (John 20:22).

"Love the LORD your God with all your heart and with all your soul and with all your strength" (Deuteronomy 6:5).

"Jesus replied, 'Love the Lord your God with all your heart and with all your soul and with all your mind'" (Matthew 22:37).

"Watch and pray so that you will not fall into temptation. The spirit is willing, but the flesh is weak" (Matthew 26:41).

Sower of the Seed
Some People Are Like Seed

"A farmer went out to sow his seed. As he was scattering the seed, some fell along the path, and the birds came and ate it up."[206]

"Some fell on rocky places, where it did not have much soil. It sprang up quickly because the soil was shallow."[207]

"But when the sun came up, the plants were scorched, and they withered because they had no root."[208]

"Other seed fell among thorns, which grew up and choked the plants."[209]

"Still other seed fell on good soil, where it produced a crop a hundred, sixty or thirty times what was sown. Whoever has ears, let them hear."[210]

"Listen then to what the parable of the sower means."[211]

"When anyone hears the message about the kingdom of God and does not understand it, the evil one [Satan] comes and snatches away the word what was sown in their heart, so that they may not believe and be saved. This is the seed sown along the path."[212]

---

[206] Matthew 13:3–4; Mark 4:3–4
[207] Matthew 13:5
[208] Matthew 13:6
[209] Matthew 13:7
[210] Matthew 13:8–9
[211] Matthew 13:18
[212] Matthew 13:19

"The seed falling on rocky ground refers to someone who hears the word and at once receives it with joy."[213]

"But since they have no root, they last only a short time. When trouble or persecution comes because of the word, they quickly fall away."[214]

"The seed falling among the thorns refers to someone who hears the word, but the worries of this life and the deceitfulness of wealth choke the word, making it unfruitful."[215]

"But the seed falling on good soil refers to someone who hears the word and understands it. This is the one who produces a crop, yielding a hundred, sixty or thirty times what was sown."[216]

This story helps you understand why it is so important to renew your mind to the word of God and only the born-again believer will get understanding.

"Jesus told them, 'The secret of the kingdom of God has been given to you. But to those on the outside [unbelievers] everything is said in parables so that, they may be ever seeing but never perceiving, and ever hearing but never understanding'."[217]

[213] Matthew 13:20
[214] Matthew 13:21
[215] Matthew 13:22
[216] Matthew 13:23
[217] Mark 4:11–12

Who Is Your Father?
God or the Devil?

Parable of the Wheat and Weeds

The kingdom of heaven is like a man who sowed good seed in his field. But while everyone was sleeping, his enemy came and sowed weeds among the wheat, and went away. When the wheat sprouted and formed heads, then the weeds also appeared. The owner's servants came to him and said, 'Sir, didn't you sow good seed in your field? Where then did the weeds come from?' An enemy did this; he replied. The servants asked him 'Do you want us to go and pull them up?' No, he answered, because while you are pulling the weeds, you may up-root the wheat with them. Let both grow together until the harvest. At that time, I will tell the harvesters: First collect the weeds and tie them in bundles to be burned; then gather the wheat and bring it into my barn. (Matthew 13:24–30)

"Jesus's disciples ask him to explain to them the parable about the weeds in the field" (Matthew 13:36).

"He answered, 'The one who sowed the good seed is the Son of Man'" (Matthew 13:37).

"The field is the world, and the good seed stands for the people of the kingdom. The weeds are the people of the evil one" (Matthew 13:38).

"You belong to your father, the devil, and you want to carry out your father's desires. He was a murderer from the beginning, not holding to the truth, for there is no truth in him. When he lies, he speaks his native language, for he is a liar and the father of lies" (John 8:44).

"Yet because I tell the truth, you do not believe me!" (John 8:45).

"This is how we know who the children of God are and who the children of the devil are: Anyone who does not do what is right is not God's child, nor is anyone who does not love their brother and sister" (1 John 3:10).

"And the enemy who sows them is the devil. The harvest is the end of the age, and the harvesters are angels" (Matthew 13:39).

"As Jesus was sitting on the Mount of Olives, the disciples came to him privately. Tell us, they said, when will this happen, and what will be the sign of your coming and of the end of the age?" (Matthew 24:3).

"And teaching them to obey everything I have commanded you. And surely, I am with you always, to the very end of the age" (Matthew 28:20).

"Then another angel came out of the temple and called in a loud voice to him who was sitting on the cloud, 'Take your sickle and reap, because the time to reap has come, for the harvest of the earth is ripe'" (Revelation 14:15).

"As the weeds are pulled up burned in the fire, so it will be at the end of the age" (Matthew 13:40).

"The Son of Man will send out his angels, and they will weed out of his kingdom everything that causes sin and all who do evil" (Matthew 13:41).

"And he will send his angels with a loud trumpet call, and they will gather his elect from the four winds, from one end of the heavens to the other" (Matthew 24:31).

"They will throw them into the blazing furnace, where there will be weeping and gnashing of teeth" (Matthew 13:42).

"But the subjects of the kingdom will be thrown outside, into the darkness, where there will be weeping and gnashing of teeth" (Matthew 8:12).

"Then the righteous will shine like the sun in the kingdom of their Father. Whoever has ears, let them hear" (Matthew 13:43).

"Those who are wise will shine like the brightness of the heavens, and those who leads many to righteousness, like the stars for ever and ever" (Daniel 12:3).

Righteous from the Unrighteous
Separation of the Sheep from the Goats

"When the Son of Man comes in his glory, and all the angels with him, he will sit on his glorious throne" (Matthew 25:31).

"For the Son of Man is going to come in his Father's glory with his angels, and then he will reward each person according to what they have done" (Matthew 16:27).

"Jesus said to them, Truly I tell you, at the renewal of all things, when the Son of Man sits on his glorious throne, you who have followed me will also sit on twelve thrones, judging the twelve tribes of Israel" (Matthew 19:28).

"All the nations will be gathered before him, and he will separate the people one from the another as a shepherd separates the sheep from the goats" (Matthew 25:32).

"And you will again see the distinction between the righteous and the wicked, between those who serve God and those who do not" (Malachi 3:18).

"Then the King will say to those on his right, Come, you who are blessed by my Father; take your inheritance, the kingdom prepared for you since the creation of the world" (Matthew 25:34).

"And saying Repent, for the kingdom of heaven has come near" (Matthew 3:2).

"Blessed are the poor in spirit, for theirs is the kingdom of heaven" (Matthew 5:3).

"Blessed are those who are persecuted because of righteousness, for theirs is the kingdom of heaven" (Matthew 5:10).

"Now I commit you to God and to the word of his grace, which can build you up and give you an inheritance among all those who are sanctified" (Acts 20:32).

"I declare to you, brothers and sisters, that flesh and blood cannot inherit the kingdom of God, nor does the perishable inherit the imperishable" (1 Corinthians 15:50).

"Listen, my dear brothers and sisters has not God chosen those who are poor in the eyes of the world to be rich in faith and to inherit the kingdom he promised those who love him?" (James 2:5).

"Now we who have believed enter that rest, just as God has said" (Hebrews 4:3).

"Otherwise! Christ; would have had to suffer many times since the creation of the world. But he has appeared once for all at the culmination of the ages to do away with sin by the sacrifice of himself" (Hebrews 9:26).

"For I was hungry; and you gave me something to eat, I was thirsty, and you gave me something to drink, I was a stranger and you invited me in, I needed clothes and you clothed me, I was sick, and you looked after me, I was in prison and you came to visit me" (Matthew 25:35–36).

"Do not forget to show hospitality to strangers, for by so doing some people have shown hospitality to angels without knowing it" (Hebrews 13:2).

"Suppose a brother or a sister is without clothes and daily food. If one of you says to them, Go, in peace keep warm and well fed, but does nothing about their physical needs, what good is it?" (James 2:15–16).

"Then the righteous will answer him, Lord, when did we see you hungry and feed you, or thirsty and give you something to drink? When did we see you a stranger and invite you in, or needing clothes and clothe you? When did we see you sick or in prison and go to visit you? The King will reply, Truly I tell you, whatever you did for one of the least of these brothers and sisters of mine, you did for me" (Matthew 25:37–40).

"Whoever is kind to the poor lends to the LORD, and he will reward them for what they have done" (Proverbs 19:17).

"Anyone who welcomes you welcomes me, and anyone who welcomes me welcomes the one who sent me" (Matthew 10:40).

"And if anyone gives even a cup of cold water to one of these little ones who is my disciple, truly I tell you, that person will certainly not lose their reward" (Matthew 10:42).

"God is not unjust; he will not forget your work and the love you have shown him as you have helped his people and continue to help them" (Hebrews 6:10).

"Then he will say to those on his left, 'Depart, from me you who are cursed, into the eternal fire prepared for the devil and his angels'" (Matthew 25:41).

"Then I will tell them plainly, I never knew you. Away from me, you evildoers!" (Matthew 7:23).

"And they will go out and look on the dead bodies of those who rebelled against me; the worms that eat them will not die, the fire that burns them will not be quenched and they will be loathsome to all mankind" (Isaiah 66:24).

"For if God did not spare angels when they sinned, but sent them to hell, putting them in chains of darkness to be held for judgment" (2 Peter 2:4).

"For I was hungry, and you gave me nothing to eat, I was thirsty, and you gave me nothing to drink, I was a stranger, and you did not invite me in, I needed clothes and you did not clothe me, I was sick and in prison and you did not look after me. They also will answer, Lord, when did we see you hungry or thirsty or a stranger or needing clothes or sick or in prison, and did not help you? He will reply, Truly I tell you, whatever you did not do for one of the least of these, you did not do for me" (Matthew 25:42–45).

"Whoever oppresses the poor shows contempt for their Maker, but whoever is kind to the needy honors God" (Proverbs 14:31).

"Whoever mocks the poor shows contempt for their Maker; whoever gloats over disaster will not go unpunished" (Proverbs 17:5).

"Then they will go away to eternal punishment, but the righteous to eternal life" (Matthew 25:46).

"And everyone who has left houses or brothers or sisters or father or mother or wife or children or fields for my sake will receive a hundred times as much and will inherit eternal life" (Matthew 19:29).

"That everyone who believes may have eternal life in him" (John 3:15).

"For God so loved the world that he gave his one and only Son, that whoever believes in him shall not perish but have eternal life" (John 3:16).

"Whoever believes in the Son has eternal life, but whoever rejects the Son will not see life, for God's wrath remains on them" (John 3:36).

"For you granted him authority over all people that he might give eternal life to all those you have given him" (John 17:2).

"Now this is eternal life: that they know you, the only true God, and Jesus Christ, whom you have sent" (John 17:3).

"Whoever sows to please their flesh, from the flesh will reap destruction; whoever sows to please the Spirit, from the Spirit will reap eternal life" (Galatians 6:8).

BELIEVING RIGHT
LEADS TO
LOVING RIGHT
LEADS TO
LIVING RIGHT
REST IN THE FATHER'S LOVE FOR YOU

THE
WATER
IS
THE
SPIRIT
AND
WORD
OF
GOD

He saved us through the washing of rebirth
and renewal by the Holy Spirit.

—Titus 3:5

The Water Is the Spirit and Word of God

I would like for you to imagine two water hoses one with no holes in them untangled and the other with holes in them and knotted and tangled. We are going to use the illustration of the water hoses in reference to your life. The Word of God is the water that flows through the hoses. If you do not get all the junk out of your life by renewing your mind with the word of God, believing and receiving in it, you will continue to live a defeated life even as a Christian. The Bible teaches in John 4:7–15,

> When a Samaritan woman came to draw water from the well, Jesus had a conversation telling her if you knew the gift of God and who it is that asks you for a drink you would have asked him, and he would have given you living water. Sir, the woman said, you have nothing to draw with and the well is deep. Where can you get this living water? Are you greater than our father Jacob, who gave us the well and drank from it himself, as did also his sons and livestock? Jesus answered, "Everyone who drinks this will be thirsty again, but whoever drinks the water I give them will never thirst. Indeed, the water I give them will become in them a spring of water welling up to eternal life." The woman said to him,

"Sir, give me this water so that I won't get thirsty and have to keep coming here to draw water."

The water is the Spirit of God, which is the Word as well.

> My people have committed two sins they have forsaken me, the spring of living water. (Jeremiah 2:13)

> On the last and greatest day of the festival, Jesus stood and said in a loud voice, "Let anyone who is thirsty come to me and drink. Whoever believes in me, as Scripture has said, rivers of living water will flow from within them. By this he meant the Spirit, whom those who believed in him were later to receive. Up to that time the Spirit had not been given since Jesus had not yet been glorified. (John 7:37–39)

I wanted you to see these scriptures to show you how the Spirit is the water that flows through you when you receive the word of God and apply it to your life. Allowing the water to flow pushes out all the junk in your life, then changes will begin to take place that you and others will see.

Getting the Junk Out of Your Life
Things That Clog Up the Hose

The water is the Spirit and the Word of God which is designed to cleanse you. The choices and decision you make can cause the hose to clog and slow the flow of the water in your life.

"Every good and perfect gift is from above, coming down from the Father of the heavenly lights, who does not change like shifting shadows" (James 1:17).

"Don't you know that you yourselves are God's temple and that God's Spirit dwells in your midst?" (1 Corinthians 3:16).

"The body, however, is not meant for sexual immorality but for the Lord, and the Lord for the body" (1 Corinthians 6:13).

"If anyone destroys God's temple, God will destroy that person; for God's temple is sacred, and you are that temple" (1 Corinthians 3:17).

"The flesh desires what is contrary to the Spirit" (Galatians 5:17).

"So you must get rid of these things out of your life. Put to death, therefore, whatever belongs to your earthly nature" (Colossians 3:5).

"The acts of the flesh: sexual immorality, impurity and debauchery; idolatry and witchcraft; hatred, discord, jealousy, fits of rage, selfish ambition, dissensions, factions and envy; drunkenness, orgies, and the like" (Galatians 5:19–21).

"Let us throw off everything that hinders and the sin that so easily entangles" (Hebrews 12:1).

"Those who do live like this cannot inherit the kingdom of God and will not experience the Spirit flowing through them" (Galatians 5:21).

"Even though you are born-again, it can still *stop* the flow of the Spirit because you are living worldly. That is the hose which have the holes and knots in them. Remember as believer of Christ, we are in this world but not of it" (John 17:14).

"We live by the faith of the Spirit of God and not by sight" (2 Corinthians 5:7).

"Walk by the Spirit, and you will not gratify the desires of the flesh" (Galatians 5:16).

"Now if you desire change in your life, start applying the Word of God and you will see it. The Scripture teaches us that those who trust in him will not be ashamed" (Romans 10:11).

Then others will begin to see the growth and changes take place in your life.

"Let us draw near to God with a sincere heart and with the full assurance that faith brings, having our hearts sprinkled to cleanse us from a guilty conscience and having our bodies washed with pure water" (Hebrews 10:22).

"But you were washed, you were sanctified, you were justified in the name of the Lord Jesus Christ and by the Spirit of our God" (1 Corinthians 6:11).

"For everyone born of God overcomes the world. This is the victory that has overcome the world, even our faith" (1 John 5:4).

Reference Scriptures

"For the Lamb at the center of the throne will be their shepherd; he will lead them to springs of living water" (Revelation 7:17).

"Let us draw near to God with a sincere heart and with the full assurance that faith brings, having our hearts sprinkled to cleanse us from a guilty conscience and having our bodies washed with pure water" (Hebrews 10:22).

"Husbands, love your wives, just as Christ loved the church and gave himself up for her to make her holy, cleansing her by the washing with water through the word" (Ephesians 5:25–26).

"For I will pour water on the thirsty land, and streams on the dry ground; I will pour out my Spirit on your offspring, and my blessing on your descendants" (Isaiah 44:3).

"For with you is the fountain of life, in your light we see light" (Psalm 36:9).

"You, God are my God, earnestly I seek you; I thirst for you, my whole being longs for you, in a dry and parched land where there is no water" (Psalm 63:1).

"Wash and make yourselves clean. Take your evil deeds out of my sight; stop doing wrong" (Isaiah 1:16).

"Jesus declared, 'I am the bread of life. Whoever comes to me will never go hungry, and whoever believes in me will never be thirsty'" (John 6:35).

LIVE
OUT
YOUR
LOVE!
LIVE
OUT
YOUR
DREAMS!

For everyone born of God overcomes the world.
This is the victory that has overcome the world, even our faith.

—1 John 5:4

YOU
ARE
BLESSED
TO
BE
A
BLESSING

The Father Has Given You Authority through Jesus Christ (The Keys Represent Authority)

"God said, 'Let Us (Father, Son, and Holy Spirit) make mankind in Our image, after Our likeness, and let them have complete authority over the fish of the sea, the birds of the air, cattle, and over all the earth, and over everything that creeps upon the earth'" (Genesis 1:26 AMP).

"What is mankind that you are mindful of them, human beings that you care for them? You have made them a little lower than the angels and crowned them with glory and honor. You made them rulers over the works of your hands; you put everything under their feet" (Psalm 8:4–6 NIV).

"I will give you the keys of the kingdom of heaven; and whatever you bind (declare to be improper and unlawful) on earth must be what is already bound in heaven; and whatever you loose (declared lawful) on earth must be what is already loosed in heaven" (Matthew 16:19 AMP).

"Then Jesus came to them (his disciples) and said, "All authority in heaven and on earth has been given to me" (Matthew 28:18 NIV).

"I have given you authority to trample on snakes and scorpions and to overcome all the power of the enemy; nothing will harm you" (Luke 10:19 NIV).

Scriptures to Meditate On

"Blessed are those who fear the lord, who find great delight in his commands" (Psalm 112:1).

"But seek first his kingdom and his righteousness, and all these things will be given to you as well" (Matthew 6:33).

"Unless the Lord builds the house, the builders labor in vain. Unless the lord watches over the city, the guards stand watch in vain" (Psalm 127:1).

"Take delight in the lord, and he will give you the desires of your heart" (Psalm 37:4).

"Their children will be mighty in the land; the generation of the upright will be blessed" (Psalm 112:2).

"Children are a heritage from the lord, offspring a reward from him" (Psalm 127:3).

"And all your children shall be taught by the lord and great shall be the peace of your children" (Isaiah 54:13).

"Wealth and riches are in their houses, and their righteousness endures forever" (Psalm 112:3).

"The lord shall increase you more and more, you and your children" (Psalm 115:14).

"Your word is a lamp for my feet, a light on my path" (Psalm 119:105).

"No weapon that is formed against you shall prosper" (Isaiah 54:17).

"Trust in the lord with all your heart and lean not on your own understanding" (Proverbs 3:5).

"In all your ways submit to him, and he will make your paths straight" (Proverbs 3:6).

"The thief comes only to steal and kill and destroy; I have come that they may have life and have it to the full" (John 10:10).

"Those who hope in the lord will renew their strength. They will soar on wings like eagles; they will run and not grow weary; they will walk and not be faint" (Isaiah 40:31).

"For the lord is good and his love endures forever; his faithfulness continues through all generations" (Psalm 100:5).

"I can do all things through Christ who gives me strength" (Philippians 4:13).

"And my God will meet all my needs according to the riches of his glory in Christ Jesus" (Philippians 4:19).

It's
Love
from the Beginning
and
It's
Love
to
the
End

You
Were
Created
by
Love
for
Love
in
Love
To
Love

Prayer for Salvation

If you would like to receive all that God the Father has for you by believing in Jesus, making him your Lord and Savior, please pray this prayer:

Thank you, Father, for sending your beloved Son Jesus, to die on the cross for me. And thank you, Lord Jesus, for obeying the Father's will. Your precious blood washes me clean of every sin. I confess you as my Lord and my Savior, now and forever. I believe that the Father has raised you from the dead and you are alive today. Because of your finished work, I am a beloved child of God the Father and heaven is my home. Hallelujah! Amen.

> If you declare with your mouth, Jesus is Lord, and believe in your heart that God raised him from the dead, you will be saved. (Romans 10: 9, 10)

> For it is with your heart that you believe and are justified, and it is with your mouth that you profess your faith and are saved.

THE
FATHER
OF
LOVE
HAS
A
PLAN
FOR
YOUR
LIFE

"For I know the plans I have for you," declares
the Lord, "plans to prosper you and not to harm
you, plans to give you hope and a future."

—Jeremiah 29:11

About the Author

Darlene Dennard is a wife and mother of four beautiful children and grandchildren. I have known her for well over ten years as a loyal friend and woman of God. I personally experience her spiritual growth and have been blessed and inspired by her revelation of the grace and love of God. I believe that I and anyone who reads this book will be blessed by what God has bestowed upon her heart to express through his Word and love toward others.

Jannie M. Edwards

CPSIA information can be obtained
at www.ICGtesting.com
Printed in the USA
JSHW022127160222
22956JS00001B/7